Ancestors

and Descendants of

CAPTAIN JOHN JAMES

and

ESTHER DENISON

of

Preston, Connecticut

Compiled by

CLARA PAINE OHLER

Lima, Ohio

1912

1570268

DEDICATORY

THIS BOOK IS AFFECTIONATELY DEDICATED, FIRST OF ALL, TO MY SISTER, DELIA E. PAINE, SECONDLY, TO THE MANY "COUSINS" WHOSE NAMES APPEAR IN ITS PAGES, AND WHO, I HOPE, WILL SHARE WITH ME THE PLEASURE I HAVE EXPERIENCED IN LEARNING OF THE LIVES AND DEEDS OF OUR ANCESTORS.

FOREWORD.

For many years the author has devoted much time and study to everything which our Genealogical libraries contain in reference to our common ancestors; in addition, has also spent much time and effort in correspondence with various branches of our family to obtain unpublished data and family records, that all might be properly arranged for reference by this and future generations.

Reward has come in the finding of data sufficient to make an authentic history of our forebears, and to give to each descendant, his or her proper place on the family tree.

It is a great pleasure to be able to present to you who find your names upon its branches, a glimpse of the lives of our forefathers, and to trace your descent and mine, from these valiant men and women. It is my hope that each one who reads what has been collected together in these pages, will be imbued with a desire to visit the ancient homes of his ancestors, and to so familiarize himself or herself with the full history of the colonial and revolutionary epochs with which they were connected, that they may fully appreciate the part played by their forebears in the founding and perpetuation of America.

Wherever possible, authority for records is given, so that this book may be found reliable in the preparation of application papers for ancestral societies.

The author wishes to acknowledge her appreciation of the assistance rendered by those who spared no effort to procure the family records so kindly contributed.

Index of Families

James - - - - - - - - 5

Denison - - - - - - - - 146

Lay - - - - - - - - - 162

Avery - - - - - - - - - 168

Chesebrough - - - - - - - 183

Tyler - - - - - - - - - 189

James

Across the sea, the name of James is associated with history and events of more than passing interest. From an article upon the James family recently published by the Frank Allaben Genealogical Co., we make the following extract· "One branch of the family traces its pedigree back to the Lady Godiva of Tennyson's poem." A line of baronets of the name of James, originally bore the name of Haestricht, the designation of an ancient lordship near Utrecht, Holland.

Roger, son of Jacob von Haestricht, went to Kent, England, in the time of Henry VIII, and was known by the name of Roger Jacob, or Roger, son of Jacob, which was finally changed to its English equivalent of James.

In Pembrokeshire, there is a tradition that an estate there was owned by thirteen successive proprietors, all bearing the name of William James. Langley Hall, in Berkshire, is one James home, while branches of the family have been well represented in Dorset, Somerset, Lancaster, Essex, Kent and Worcester. In our own country, the family has been prominent in Virginia, Pennsylvania, New Jersey and the New England states."

A few years ago a chart of the James family was purchased, hoping that it would afford some clue to the ancestry of Captain John James. While apparently without special interest for us, the several divisions of the James family were outlined, a brief sketch of which may not be out of place. One John James founded a family in Montgomery county, Pa. Abel James, who may have been his descendant, was a mer-

chant of Philadelphia, and married Rebecca Chalkley. Their son, Chalkley James, was the founder of the Pennsylvania Historical Society.

Philip James, of Hingham, Mass, through his son Francis, left a large posterity.

William B. James, of Vermillion county, Ind., married Elizabeth Duling and was the grand father of Edmund J. James, of Philadelphia, president of the American Academy of Political and Social Service. John James of Deerfield, N. H., also left numerous descendants.

Since we know that our ancestor, Capt. John James, came from Exeter, R. I., it seems only fair to suppose that he was connected with some of the many James families who were early settlers of that state. The name was a common one at Newport, where we find record of one William James who married Susanna Martin, December 10, 1677. Record is also found of one John James of Newport. "son of William and Susannah James," who married Lydia Peckham, of Little Compton, February 12, 1729.

Among the birth records is found one of John James, "son of John and Lydia James, of Newport," who was born August 2, 1731. These records are probably taken from the South-Kingston meeting house.

Another "John James, son of John" married first, Margaret ——————, and by her had several children. He was of Richmond, R. I., where there were many James'. There is a family tradition to the effect that our Captain John James was twice married, and it is possible that he is identical with our ancestor; and that he may have removed from Richmond to Exeter, only a few miles away.

It is said that in Wales, there were two families of James, one of which was known as the "Little James"

and the other was designated as the "Big James" tribe. It is impossible to say from which one of the various James families referred to, our ancestor, Captain John James, is descended

From his stature and that of his sons, we might surmise that he was of the "Big James" tribe. However all that we really know of his history previous to his marriage at Preston, Connecticut, to Esther Denison, is the statement contained in the marriage record, that he was "formerly of Exeter, Rhode Island." A visit to Exeter, and an examination of the early records of that township, showed the residence there of various families of the name of James; and mention is made of a John James, "the son of John and Susannah James," who may have been the one for whom we sought.

However, no more definite information was obtained, and it is very doubtful if we shall ever know anything further of his antecedents.

After his marriage to Esther Denison, he continued to live in New London county, Connecticut, and the births of his children are all found upon the town records of Preston.

He was living there at the beginning of the Revolutionary war, and we find from the records of Connecticut, that he was one of the men who "marched from Connecticut towns at the Lexington alarm."

· The author recently prepared an historical article which was published in both the Connecticut Magazine and the Journal of American History.

The next few years of the life of Captain James and his family were portrayed therein and this article is therefore included in its original form.

7

"CONNECTICUT AND THE BUILDING OF THE EM-PIRE OF THE OLD NORTHWEST.

Story of the First Connecticut Pioneers who Sacrificed
Their Lives in Darkest America—Driving Back
the Barbarians and Laying the Foun-
dation of a Great Dominion.

By Mrs. Clara Paine Ohler,

Great granddaughter of Captain John James and his
wife, Esther Denison, who were in the first Indian
Massacres in the Old Northwest "

"Some time ago there appeared in the pages of
The Connecticut Magazine an article by Mabel Cassine
Holman upon the 'Hive of the Averys' and its builder,
Captain James Avery, one of the pioneers of Connect-
icut.

"Many descendants of Captain Avery, no doubt,
enjoyed the well written sketch, and were grateful
to Miss Holman for the painstaking research which
resulted in so satisfactory a portrayal of the life and
deeds of their ancestors.

"Of these, none, I am sure, were more appre-
ciative readers than one in the distant state of Ohio;
distant not only in sense of miles, but of years as well;
for more than a century has elapsed since my forebears
left the fine old state of Connecticut and turned their
steps westward toward an unknown land.

"Perhaps we, of the present generation, have
gained thereby in some respects, but in others, at
least, we have been losers; for the family traditions,
which are the natural heritage of those who live in their
ancestral state, are necessarily lost to us whose ancestors have, for several generations, been far removed,
and we are only beginning, as a people, to renew our

8

acquaintance with old New England through the medium of historical and genealogical writings, such as the sketch contributed by Miss Holman.

It is through the pleasure and benefit received from such writings that I am tempted to hope an exchange of narratives may result in mutual pleasure, and that the story of a Connecticut woman a descendant of Captain Avery, who became a pioneer of the Old Northwest Territory may be read with interest.

"Side by side with Captain James Avery fought another warrior who is prominently identified with the early history of Connecticut,—Captain George Denison.

"Coming from England when a young man, he lived for a time at Roxbury, Massachusetts, but returned to his native country and took service under Cromwell. He fought at the battle of Marston Moor and was afterwards taken prisoner, but got free and married an English girl, Miss Ann Borodell, and with her returned to New England, in the year 1645, locating for a time at Roxbury, Massachusetts, but finally removing with his family to Stonington, Connecticut, where he remained until his death, in 1694.

"We learn from the records of Massachusetts and Connecticut that "Captain George Denison was not only distinguished as a civilian, but became the most distinguished soldier of Connecticut in her early settlement, except perhaps Captain John Mason."

"In addition to their distinguished military services, both Captain Avery and Captain Denison served many terms as deputies to the General Court, and it is safe to assume that the association of the two men led to a lasting friendship between them.

"Captain Avery lived to see a closer tie than that of friendship unite two of their descendants, for we find, that, in the year 1698, William Denison, grandson

9

of Capt. George Denison, and Mary Avery, granddaughter of Capt. James Avery, were united in the holy bonds of matrimony. To this couple were born twelve children, one of whom, a son named William, was born in 1705. He married January 1, 1737, Hannah Tyler, daughter of Captain James Tyler. Eight children were born to William and Hannah (Tyler) Denison, one of whom was a daughter named Esther, whose future was destined to be closely identified with the trials of New England during the revolution, and later, with those of the Northwest Teritory during years of Indian warfare.

"Esther Denison was born on April 23, 1746, probably in the town of North Stonington. Of her early life we know little except that in 1763, at the age of seventeen, she was married to John James, and that they afterward lived both in North Stonington and Preston, Connecticut Of this period of her life, little more is known, at least to the writer, except that she became a member of the Preston Congregational church in 1767.

"Soon after her marriage came the stirring times preceding the Revolutionary War, and when the call to arms was sounded, we find the name of John James among the "Minute Men" from Connecticut who re-sponded to the "Lexington Alarm."

"We find him again enrolled as "sergeant" at the siege of New London, and feel sure that his life was devoted to the cause of liberty all through the struggle for independence, and that he was aided and encouraged in every way possible by his wife, whose patriotism in those trying times we know was worthy of her lineage.

"The close of the Revolutionary War was followed by a period of reconstruction and was a natural time

for the soldiers of the army to make radical changes; hence the movement to organize what was known as the 'Ohio Company' found ample support in the New England states.

"It is nearly a century and a quarter since General Rufus Putnam and his brother officers met at the 'Bunch of Grapes' tavern in Boston on April 25, 1786, and organized the 'Ohio Company of Associates,' and it is a matter of history that Manasseh Cutler, of Connecticut, 'representing soldiers of the Revolutionary Army organized as the Ohio Company of Associates, purchased from the board of treasury of the United States, on authority granted by the Continental Congress, July 27, 1787, a million and a half acres of those waste and vacant lands.'

"The first body of settlers, forty-eight in number, headed by General Rufus Putnam, landed at the mouth of the Muskingum River, on April 7, 1788, and christened their new home in honor of the French queen, Marietta.

"This has come to be known as the landing of the 'Mayflower II,' and has been made the subject of song and story almost as often as its famous predecessor.

"General St. Clair, first governor of the Northwest Territory, arrived at Fort Harmar on July 9, 1788, and upon his official entry into Marietta, on July 10th, civil government was established.

"For a detailed account of these early settlers, I am indebted to Dr. Hildreth, their first historian. From his ancient records I learn that, during the first winter of their occupation of the Northwest Territory, the directors of the Ohio Company sent out exploiting partes to examine their purchase.

"They reported a fine tract of land on the right

.

bank of the Ohio river commencing near the mouth of the Kanawha River and extending down the Ohio four or five miles. It included a rich strip of bottom land about three miles in length by one-third of a mile in width. This was divided into farms about forty rods wide and extending back to the hills which rose to an elevation of a hundred feet in the background.

"This beautiful spot was named 'Belle-prairie' or 'Beautiful meadow,' but the name has been shortened by usage into Belpre.

"The second settlement was composed of about forty associates, the largest portion of whom had served as officers in the Revolutionary War, and when the army disbanded, retired with a brevet promotion.

"To a stranger, it seemed curious that every house he passed should be occupied by a commissioned officer. It is said that 'No settlement ever formed west of the mountains contained so many men of real merit, sound practical sense, and refined manner.

" 'They had been in the school of Washington and were nearly or quite all of them, acquainted with that great and good man. All of the families in the Belpre settlement had received the advantage of the common schools in New England and some had been more liberally educated. They were habituated to industry and economy and brought up under the influence of morality and religion. They had been selected to lead their countrymen to battle and to defend their rights, not for their physical strength, but for their moral standing and superior intellect.

" 'In addition to these advantages they had also received a second education in the Army of the Revolution, where they heard the precepts of wisdom and witnessed the examples of bravery and fortitude, learning at the same time, the necessity of subordina-

12

tion to law and good order in promoting the happiness and prosperity of mankind.' (From manuscript notes of Judge Barker.)

"Most of the Belpre associates passed the first winter in Marietta, moving onto their farms in the spring of 1789; several families, however, did not occupy their lands until the following year. The Ohio Associates came from New England in four companies, several months apart, and covering in all about two years

"In the last company I find my great grandfather, Captain John James, and family. The latter consisted of his wife, Esther Denison James, and ten children.

"The settlement of Belpre consisted at this time of the forty families before mentioned, who lived in log houses near the river bank; into one of these Captain James and his family moved and began the life of pioneers. The immense forest trees were cut down and a rail fence was built in the rear of the fields to protect the crops from the cattle. The houses were connected by paths which ran through the fields, and a number of springs of pure water afforded comfort to the settlers.

"Scarcely were they thus comfortably housed than they were brought face to face with a famine caused by the rotting of the crops, and the history of the 'starving time' of the Pilgrims in Old Plymouth was repeated on the banks of the Ohio. No sooner had this calamity been overcome than the settlers were asasiled by one yet more dire.

"From the records of Washington county we learn that a new association had been formed in the fall of 1790, locating upon a tract of land known as 'Big Bottom,' which had attracted attention from its great beauty and richness.

"This association numbered thirty-six members, only eighteen, however, going originally to the new settlement. All of these were young men with the exception of a hunter who accompanied them, taking with him his wife and children. Among the number was William James, a son of Captain James.

"The older members of the settlement tried in vain to dissuade them from making the venture, believing that the Indians were inclined to be hostile. Unheeded, however, were the warnings, and a block-house of good dimensions was erected upon the banks of the Muskingum River, several miles distant from the other settlements. Two cabins were also built about twenty rods from the block-house, one occupied by Francis and Isaac Choate, and the other by Eleazer Bullard and his brother Asa.

"With all the rashness of youth and inexperience, the young men, believing that they were safe from any possible attack by the Indians in the winter season, failed to enclose their block-house with palisades, or make any system of defense, such as the setting of sentinels to watch for danger. By their carelessness, they thus brought upon themselves the attack which is known as the 'Massacre of Big Bottom,' and which was followed by years of Indian warfare. The following account of the massacre is taken from the history of Washington county:

"One evening, in the winter of 1790-1791, the inmates of the block-house were gathered around the large fire place. Some were engaged in preparing the evening meal, while others warmed themselves by the genial blaze, when the door was thrown suddenly open, and a volley of musketry poured death into their midst. Several fell lifeless to the floor, while one, Zebulon Throop, who was bending over a frying pan in which

14

he was cooking venison for supper, sank down upon the blazing logs. The shots were fired from without, while one of the Indians, who had burst the door, held it open.

"No sooner had the guns been emptied than, with a fiendish yell, the savages leaped through the smoke to finish with their tomahawks the butchery begun with powder and ball. So sudden and so fierce was the onslaught that little resistance could be made, and one after another the inmates of the block-house were dispatched. Only one Indian was wounded and he by the wife of the hunter. She had witnessed the brutal slaying of her children; had seen them scalped and thrown into the blazing fire, and, with the courage of a madman, she seized an axe and struck wildly at one of the murderers.

"The blow came near proving fatal at the instant, but was quickly avenged by the companion of the assaulted one, who, coming up behind her, as the woman was again raising the heavy axe to strike, cleft her skull with his tomahawk. The air was filled with the wild yells of the Indians, the moans of the dying, the agonizing shrieks and the supplications of those on whom the cruel death-blow had not yet descended.

"All were quickly dispatched except Philip, a son of Colonel William Stacey, who, during the excitement of the massacre, had cowered down in a corner of the room and pulled some bedclothes over himself. He was discovered by an Indian who was searching for articles of plunder. As soon as his hiding place was revealed, a tomahawk was raised to kill him and the terrified boy, who then threw himself at the feet of the murderer, would have been dispatched in spite of his piteous entreaties if another Indian had not interposed and saved him.

15

"Besides the boy, only two men who occupied one of the cabins near by, escaped. The names of the killed were as follows. Ezra Putnam, Zebulon Throop, John Stacey, John Camp. Jonathan Farewell, James Couch, John Clark, William James, Isaac Meeks, his wife and children.

"Two days after the massacre Captain Rogers led a company of men to Big Bottom. They met a company from Marietta headed by Anselm Tupper, and together they found that the Indians, after taking the lives of the twelve pioneers, had pulled up the flooring, piled it over the bodies of their victims, and set fire to the whole.

"The block-house had not long been built, was constructed of birch logs and had been only partially consumed Most of the bodies, however, were so disfigured by the tomahawks and the fire as to be unrecognizable. William James' remains were identified by his great size. He had measured six feet four inches in stature and was of massive build.

"The ground being frozen very hard, a grave was dug within the walls of the block-house, where it had been prevented from freezing by the fire, and there the victims of the savages were buried side by side as they had fallen, and the charred charnel house remained in the now solitary and soundless forest as a grim shelter from the rain and snow—a desolate monument to the memory of the brave, unfortunate pioneers who slept beneath it, and a landmark to the hunter or scout, who passing it afar off, had a horrible suggestion of the fate which might be his.

"No attempt was again made to form a settlement here, until after the Greenville Treaty of 1795, for the massacre was the 'bloodiest in the annals of the first settlement of Ohio and it not only terrified the inhab-

itants of Marietta and Belpre, but sent a thrill of horror into all of the border settlements of Virginia and Pennsylvania, which left them accustomed as they were to Indians atrocities, filled with foreboding for many a day.'

"Meanwhile word of the massacre had been carried to Marietta, and I now quote at length from the long-neglected records of Dr Hildreth.

'The county seat of quarter sessions met at Marietta on the first Monday in January. A considerable amount of the most active men were called there to attend as jurors, witnesses etc. As it was a laborious task to get there by water, in canoes, many of them went up on Saturday and Sunday preceding. The court had barely opened Monday, when word was brought of the sacking and slaughter of Big Bottom. It was immediately adjourned and the men returned to their homes full of anxiety for the fate of their own families. Notices had been sent to the settlers at Belpre from Wolf Creek Mills at the same time it was sent to Marietta. The woman and children suffered much from fear, expecting every hour that the Indians would attack them.

"The inhabitants were scattered along the river bank, living in their log cabins, without any preparation for defense, not expecting an Indian war, as a treaty had been made with them only two years before. Captain Jonathan Stone, at the upper settlement had built a small block-house for his dwelling and into this all the women and children were gathered on Monday night. On Tuesday there was a general muster of all the heads of families, to consult on what was best to be done. They decided on collecting them all together, about thirty in number, at the middle settlement, where Colonel Cushing and Colonel Bat-

telle had already built two large log houses, and erected a spacious, strong, and well arranged garrison, sufficient for the accommodation of all the inhabitants The spot selected was on the bank of the river, about half a mile below the 'Bluff,' and nearly against the center of Backus' Island. A swamp about six rods back from the Ohio, protected its rear, while the river defended the front. The upper and lower ends opened into a smooth, level bottom, suitable for a road by which to enter or depart from the garrison. The work was commenced the first week in January, and was prosecuted with the utmost energy, as their lives, apparently, depended on its completion

"As fast as the block-houses were built, the families moved into them. They were thirteen in number, arranged in two rows, with a wide street between. The basement story was in general twenty feet square, and the upper twenty-two feet, thus projecting over the lower one, and forming a defense from which to protect the doors and windows below, in an attack. They were built of round logs a foot in diameter, and the interstices nicely chinked and pointed with mortar. The doors and window shutters were made of thick oak planks or puncheons, and secured with stout bars of wood on the inside. The large timbers were hauled with ox-teams, of which they had several yokes, while the lighter for the roofs, gates, etc., were dragged along on hand sleds by men. The drawing was much facilitated by a few inches of snow which covered the ground. The pickets were made of quartered oak timber growing on the plain back of the garrison, formed from trees about a foot in diameter, fourteen feet in length, and set four feet deep in the ground, leaving them ten feet high, over which no enemy could mount without a ladder. The smooth side was set

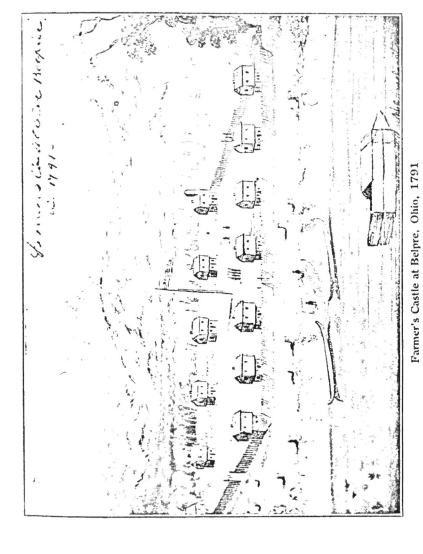

Farmer's Castle at Belpre, Ohio, 1791

outward, and the palisades strengthened and kept in their places by stout ribbons, or wall pieces, pinned to them with three-inch nails on the inside The spaces between the houses were filled up with pickets, and occupied three or four times the width of th houses, forming a continuous wall or inclosure, about eighty rods in length and six rods wide. The palisades on the river side, filled the whole space and projected over the edge of the bank leaning on rails and posts set to support them They were sloped in this manner for the admission of air during the heat of summer. Gates of stout timber were placed in the east and west ends of the garrison, opening in the middle, for the egress and ingress of teams and to take in the cattle in an attack. A still wider gate opened near the center of the back wall, for the hauling in of wood, and all were secured with strong, heavy bars. Two or three smaller ones, called water gates, were placed on the river side, as all their water was procured from the Ohio. When there were signs of Indians discovered by the spies, the domestic animals were driven within the gates at night. At sunset all the avenues were closed.

"Every house was filled with families; and as new settlers arrived occasionally during the war, some houses contained three or four. The corner block-houses, on the back side of the garrison, were provided with watch towers, running up eight feet above the roof, where a sentry was constantly kept. When the whole was completed, the inmates of the station called it "Farmer's Castle," a name very appropriate, as it was built and occupied by farmers. The directors of the Ohio Company, with their characteristic bene-ficence, paid the expense of erecting three of the block-houses, and the money was distributed among the laborers. The view of the castle from the Ohio River

was very picturesque and imposing; looking like a small fortified city amidst the surrounding wilderness During the war, there were about seventy able bodied men mustered on the roll for military duty, and the place assumed that of a regular besieged fort, as in fact it was a great portion of the time, the Indians watching in small parties, more or less constantly, for a chance to kill or capture inhabitants when they least expected it. At sunrise the roll was called by the orderly sergeant, and if any man had overslept in the morning, or neglected to answer to his name, the penalty was fixed at the cutting out of a stump of a tree to the level with the ground, they being scattered thickly over the surface inclosed with the castle. This penalty was rigidly exacted, so that few stumps remained at the close of the war. A regular commander was appointed, with suitable subalterns

"Major Nathan Goodale was the first captain, and held that post until he moved into his own garrison in 1793, when Colonel Cushing took the command. The flag staff stood a few yards west of the back gate, near the house of Colonel Cushing, on which floated the stars and stripes of the Union Near the flag staff was a large iron howitz, or swivel gun, mounted on a plaform incased in wood, hooped with iron bands and painted to resemble a six pounder. It was so adjusted as to revolve on a socket, and thus point to any part of the works. During the spring and summer months, when there was any probability of Indians being in the vicinity, it was fired regularly, morning and evening. It could be heard distinctly for several miles around, especially up and down the Ohio; the banks and hills adjacent, re-echoing the report in a wonderful manner. This practice no doubt kept the Indians in awe, and warned them not to approach a post whose inmates

were habitually watchful, and so well prepared to defend themselves. Around this spot it was customary for the loungers and newcomers to assemble, to discuss the concerns of the castle and tell the news of the day, while passing away the many idle hours that must necessarily fall to the lot of a community confined to such narrow limits. It was also the rallying point in case of an assault, and the spot where the muster roll was called morning and evening. The spies and rangers here made report of the discoveries to the commandant; in short it was the 'place d'armes' of Farmers' Castle.

"In the upper room of every house was kept a large cask, or hogs-head, constantly filled with water, to be used only in case of a fire, either from accident, or from an attack by the Indians. It was a part of the duty of the officer of the day to inspect every house, and see that the cask was well filled. Another duty was to prevent any stack of grain or fodder being placed so near the castle as to endanger the safety of the buildings, should the Indians set them on fire, or afford a shelter in time of assault. They also inspected the gates, pickets, and houses, to see that all were in repair and well secured at night. They received despatches from abroad, and sent out expresses to other stations. Their authority was absolute, and the government strictly military.

"No people ever paid more attention to the education of their children, than the descendants of the Puritans. One of the first things done by the settlers of Belpre, after they had erected their own log dwellings, was to make provision for teaching their children the rudiments of learning, reading, writing and arithmetic Bathsheba Rouse, the daughter of John Rouse, one of the emigrants from near New Bedford,

21

Mass., was employed in the summer of 1789, to teach the small children, and for several subsequent summers, she taught a school in Farmers' Castle. She is believed to the first female who ever kept a school within the present bounds of Ohio. During the winter months, a male teacher was employed for the larger boys and young women. Daniel Mayo was the first teacher in Farmers' Castle. He came from Boston, a young man, in the family of Colonel Battelle, in the fall of the year 1788, and was a graduate of Cambridge University. The school was kept in a large room of Colonel Battelle's block-house. He was a teacher for several winters, and during the summer worked at clearing and cultivating his lot of land. He married a daughter of Colonel Israel Putnam, and after the war, settled at Newport, Kentucky, where his descendants now live. Jonathan Baldwin, another educated man, also kept school a part of the time during their confinement in garrison. These schools had no public funds as at this day to aid them, but were supported from the hard earnings of the honest pioneers.

"The larger portion of the time during the war, religious services were kept up on the Sabbath, in Farmers' Castle, by Colonel E. Battelle. The people asesmbled at the large lower room in his block-house, which was provided with seats. Notice was given of the time when the exercises began by his son, Ebenezer, then a lad of fifteen or sixteen years old, and a drummer to the garrison, marching the length of the castle, up and down, beating the drum. The inmates understood the call as readily from the 'Tattoo,' as from the sound of a bell; and generally attended regularly. The meeting was opened with prayer, sometimes read from the church service, and sometimes delivered extempore,

followed by singing, at which all the New Englanders were more or less proficient. A sermon was then read from the writings of some standard divine, and the meeting closed with singing and prayer. There was usually but one service a day. Occasionally, during the war, the Rev. Daniel Story visited them and preached on the Sabbath; but these calls were rare, owing to the danger of intercourse between the settlements from the Indians. After the war his attendance was more regular, about once a month; on the three other Sabbaths, religious services were still kept up by Colonel Battelle, at a house erected on the 'Bluff,' which accommodated both the upper and middle settlements, until the time of their being able to build other and more convenient places of worship. This holy day was generally observed and honored by the inhabitants; but not with that strictness common in New England. Very few of the leading men at that day were members of any church; yet all supported religion, morality and good order.

'Here is a list of the families who lived in Farmers' Castle, at Belpre, in the year 1792.

"No. 1. Colonel Ebenezer Battelle, wife, and four chidren, viz: Cornelius, Ebenezer, Thomas and Louisa. Cornelius and Thomas, soon after the close of the war went to the West Indies, where a rich uncle put them into lucrative employment. Thomas married a daughter of Governor Livingston, of New York, and Cornelius, the daughter of a rich planter. Louisa remained single and resided in Boston, the birthplace of her mother. Ebenezer settled on a farm in Newport, in this county, and has a numerous family of children, noted for their intelligence and respectability.

"No. 2. Captain John James, wife, and ten children, from New England, viz: Susannah, Anna, Esther,

Hannah, Abigail and Polly, William, John, Thomas and Simeon, William was killed by the Indians at the sacking of Big Bottom The others all married and settled in the vicinity, either in Ohio or Virginia.

' Also Isaac Barker, wife and eight children, from near New Bedford, Mass. Michael, Isaac, Joseph, William and Timothy, Anna, Rhoda and Nancy. All of whom subsequently married and raised families, in Athens county, where Mr. Barker settled after the war.

"Also, Daniel Cogswell wife and five children. John, Abigail, Peleg, Job and Daniel. He was noted for his eccentricity and love of fun Settled after the war, below Little Hockhocking, where the children now live.

No. 3 Captain Jonatan Stone, wife and three children, from Massachusetts, viz: Benjamin Franklin. Samuel and Rufus Putnam—two others born after the war. He lived in the upper room while the lower was used for a work shop Benjamin Franklin settled in Belpre, where the children now live; Samuel in Licking county, and Rufus Putnam, near McConnelsville, on a farm where his children now reside.

No. 4. Colonel Nathaniel Cushing, wife and six children, from Boston, Mass, viz: Nathaniel, Henry, Varnum, Thomas, Sally and Elizabeth. These all married and settled in Ohio. Three other daughters were born after the war.

"Also, Captain Jonathan Devoll, wife, and six children, lived in the upper room of the same building, from Howland's Ferry, Rhode Island, viz. Henry, Charles, Barker, Francis, Sally and Nancy, with a nephew, Christopher Devoll, whom he adopted when a child. He was the son of Silas Devoll, captain of marines on board the ship 'Alfred,' under Commander

24

Abraham Whipple. He was taken prisoner and died in the prison ship, at New York. Christopher acted as a spy for some months near the close of the war. After the peace, he returned to Rhode Island, and followed the sea.

"No. 5. Contained three families, viz· Isaac Pierce, wife and three children, Samuel, Joseph and Phebe Joseph settled in Dayton. Ohio, and held some of the most responsible positions; Samuel became a sailor; Phebe married and settled also in Dayton Nathaniel Little. wife and one child; he settled in Newport where some of the children now live. Joseph Barker, wife, and one child; Joseph born in Belpre; after the war he settled on a farm, six miles up the Muskingum He held some of the highest offices in the county, raised a numerous family of children. who rank among the most useful and intelligent citizens in the country.

"No. 6. Major Nathan Goodale, wife, and seven children, Betsy, Cynthia. Sally, Susan, Henrietta, Timothy and Lincoln. Henrietta died of the smallpox; Timothy was a young man and served a part of the time as a ranger. He died soon after the war. The daughters all married and settled in Ohio. Lincoln studied medicine, but afterward entered into trade and settled in Columbus, where he became distinguished for his wealth. many amiable qualities, and especially his affectionate kindness to his more dependent relatives.

No. 7, in the southwest corner of the garrison, contained three families, viz: A. W. Putnam, wife and one child. William Pitt, born in the garrison; he married the daughter of Daniel Loring, Esq. Also D. Loring, wife, and seven children, Israel, Rice and Jesse, Luba, Bathsheba, Charlotte and Polly, Israel

was a young man after the war settled near Gibson's Fort, Miss., where he became very wealthy in lands; Rice and Jesse settled in Belpre, on farms; Rice held the office of associate judge of the court of common pleas, and Jesse was sheriff of the county several years. The daughters all married and settled in Ohio, where their descendants onw live. Major Oliver Rice lived in the family of Mr. Long. Captain Benjamin Miles, wife, and five children lived in the same block-house, from Ruthland, Mass., viz: Benjamin Buckminster and Hubbard, twin brothers, William, Tappan and Polly. Benjamin Buckminster settled in Athens, and followed merchandise; Tappan became a preacher of the gospel; Hubbard settled in Ilinois; and William lived in Belpre, all married with numerous descendants.

"No. 8 contained Griffin Greene, Esq., wife, and four children, from Rhode Island. Richard, Philip, Griffin and Susan; all married and settled in Ohio, but the youngest son. Phebe Green was a niece, lived with them, and married Captain Jonathan Haskell, of the army, and settled in Belpre, on a farm. Their descendants live in this country.

"No. 9 contained two families, viz: John Rouse, wife and eight children, from Rochester, Mass. Michael, Bathsheba, Cynthia, Betsy, Ruth, Stephen, Robert and Barker. The latter were twins. Robert died of the scarlet fever. These children married and settled in this county; Cynthia to the Honorable Paul Fearing and Betsy to Colonel Levi Barber. These men were highly respected, and held some of the most honorable posts, both of them having been members of congress. Their descendants are among the most respectable citizens of the state. Also Major Robert Bradford, wife and three or four children, from Plymouth, Mass. Several of these children died of scarlet fever; others

26

were born after the war and now live in Ohio.

"No. 10. Captain John Levins, wife and six children, from Killingly, Conneticut, viz: Joseph, a young man, and John a boy of ten years, Nancy, Fanny, Esther and Matilda. Nancy married Jonathan Plumer; Betsy, to Dr. Mathews, of Putnam, Ohio; Esther, to Mr. Sanford; Fanny, to Joseph Lincoln, while in garrison— he was for many years a merchant in Marietta, and an excellent man—and Matilda to John White. Also Captain William Dana, wife and eight children, from Watertown, Mass., Luther and William were young men, Edmund, Stephen, John, Charles and Augustus, Betsy, Mary and Fanny; Augustus and Fanny were born in the garrison; all these married and settled in Washington county, some in Belpre, and some in Newport, which was a colony from Belpre; Charles and John settled in Mississippi.

"Between No. 10 and ·11, there was a long low building, called the barrack, in which a small detachment of United States troops were quartered. In No. 11, Mrs. Dunham, the widow of Daniel Dunham, who died in 1791, with one son and two daughters. Simeon Wright married one of the girls, and lived with her, She was the mother of Persis, killed by the Indians. Also, Captain Israel Stone, wife and ten children, from Rutland, Massachusetts, viz. Sardine, a young man, Israel, Jasper, Augustus, B. Franklin and Columbus, Betsy married to T. Guthrie, of Newbury; Matilda to Stephen Smith, of Rainbow; Lydia to Ezra Hoyt, of Big Hockhocking; Polly to John Dodge, of Waterford; and Harriet, born in the castle, to James Knowles, of Newbury. The sons and their descendants settled and lived in Washington county.

"In No. 12 lived Benjamin Patterson, wife and six children, three of the rangers, or spies, who were

single men, viz: John Shepard, George Kerr and Mathew Kerr. This man, Patterson, served as a spy three years for the settlement at Belpre, and then moved down the river. He came from Wyoming, in Pennsylvania.

"At the period of the controversy between the state of Pennsylvania and Connecticut, relative to their conflicting claims to land on the Susquehanna river, congress appointed Timothy Pickering, of Salem, Massachusetts, a man of Spartan integrity, to go upon the ground and with others try to adjust the difficulty. While there, this same B. Patterson, with two other men took Mr. Pickering from his bed at night, and conveyed him three or four miles into the woods, and bound him fast to a white oak sapling, and left him there to die of starvation. After two or three days, Patterson's conscience so worried him that he relented, and unknown to his companions, he went and unbound him, setting him at liberty. For this outrage he left Wyoming, and fled to the state of New York, and from thence, after a time, to Marietta. It was not uncommon for such persons to visit the new settlements; but finding their characters after a time following on after them they proceeded further down the river. (MS. Notes of Judge Barker.)

"Benoni Hurlburt, wife and four children lived in the same house at the time of his death. His family settled in Amestown, Athens county, where his descendants now live

"No. 13. Colonel Alexander Oliver, wife and eleven children, from the west part of Massachusetts, viz: Launcelot, a young man, Alexander, John and David. They settled in Ohio. Two of Alexander's sons are now preachers of the gospel in the Methodist church. David studied medicine and settled in the

western part of Ohio. The daughters were named, and married as follows, viz: Lucretia, to Levi Munsel, and lived several years in Marietta; his son Leander, was the first man born in Ohio who had a seat in the legislature. Betsy, to Honorable Daniel Symmes, of Cincinnati; he was the first register in the United States land office at that place. Sally, married to Major Austin, of the United States army, and settled in Cincinnati. Lucretia, to George Putnam, son of Colonel Israel Putnam. Mehala to Calvin Shepard, son of Colonel Shepard, of Marietta. He was cashier of the Miami Exporting Company Bank, and his son, R. O. is said to be the first preacher in the Methodist church who was born in Ohio. He is now an elder. Mary, to Oliver Wing, of Adams, in this county The descendants of Colonel Oliver rank with the most active, useful and wealthy citizens of Ohio.

"In No. 13 also lived Daniel Bent, wife and four children, from Rutland, Massachusetts, viz: Nahum, Daniel, Dorcas, and one other daughter married to Joel Oaks, of Newbury. Dorcas married William Dana, of Newport. Some of their descendants are living in this county, and some in Missouri. Silas Bent, Esq., the oldest son of the colonel, and wife, also lived there with two or three children. He was one of the judges of the common pleas, appointed by Governor St. Clair. After the purchase of Louisiana he removed to St Louis, and was employed in surveying the United States lands. One of his sons became the head of a fur trader's company, and established a fort high up on the Arkansas river. Elijah Pixley, wife and two children from Wyoming. He served a part of the time as drummer for the garrison, and was a celebrated maker of drums, using for this purpose a block of sassafras wood, which made a very light and neat article.

"Several other families lived in Farmers' Castle for a short time and then proceeded down the river, but the above list contains nearly all the permanent and substantial head of families who settled in Belpre in 1789 and 1790.

"Joshua Fleehart, wife, and four children, lived in a small cabin east of block-house No. 3. He was a noted hunter, and supplied the garrison with fresh meat. Soon after the war closed, he moved nearer to the frontiers, where he could follow hunting and trapping to better advantage. One of his hunting adventures is related in the transactions of the year 1794.

'During the long and tedious confinement of the inhabitants of the garrison, various were the modes sought out to make the time pass as happily as their circumstances would allow. The sports of the young men and boys consisted of games at ball, foot races, wrestling, and leaping, at all of which the larger number were adepts Foot races were especially encouraged, that it might give them an advantage in their contests with the Indians. Those of a more refined character, in which both sexes could participate, consisted chiefly in dancing. Parties of young people from Campus Martius and Fort Harmar used to come down as often as four or five times a year, and join in their festivities. These visits were made by water. in a barge or large row boat, attended by a guard of soldiers from the fort. They brought musicians with them, who were attached to the military service. A player on the violin, from Gallipolis, named Vansan, one of the French emigrants, was celebrated for his musical talents, and always accompanied the young men from that place in their visits to Farmers' Castle, where they were very welcome visitors. It is true, they did not always abound in nice cakes and rich wines;

but they treated their guests with the best they had, while the hilarity and cheerful looks of the company made amends for all besides

"The garrison at Belpre contained about twenty young females in the prime of life, with fine persons, agreeable manners, and cultivated minds. A dangerous recreation of the younger girls was to steal out of the castle in the pleasant moonlight evenings of summer, and taking possession of a canoe, push it silently up the Ohio, for a mile or more; then paddle out into the middle of the river and float gently down with the current. Some favorite singer then struck up a lively song, in which all joined their voices, making sweet melody on the calm waters of the "Belle Riviere," greatly to the delight of the young men and guards on the watch towers, but much to the alarm of their mothers, who were always in fear of the Indians. But their young and cheerful hearts thought little of the danger, but much of the amusement on the water, and a brief escape from the confinement within the walls of the garrison.

"Promenading up and down the smooth broad avenue between the rows of block-houses, about eighty rods in extent, was also another favorite summer evening recreation for the young people, while the elder ones gathered in cheerful groups at each other's dwellings, to chat on their own affairs, or the news of the day, collected as it might be from the passing boats, or the rangers in their visits to the other garrisons. Newspapers, they had few or none of, until some years after the war, the first printed in Marietta being in 1802, with the exception of a chance one sent out from a friend east of the mountains, by some moving family. After a mail route was established in 1794, they were more common. Early in autumn, partes of the young

folks visited the island on which several families resided, for the purpose of gathering grapes, papaws nuts, etc. On the heads of the island, at that day, there grew a very fine, rich, red grape, said to have been scattered there from seeds left there by the early French voyagers; it is however probable they were a native variety, fitted to grow in a sandy soil. The ground beneath the lofty trees was but little encumbered with bushes, and afforded beautiful walks, when there was no danger from the lurking savages, whose swarthy visages were mingled more or less with the thoughts of their most cheerful hours

"The 4th of July was regularly celebrated in a bowery within the walls of the garrison, where the old officers and soldiers of the revolution again recounted the trials and hardships of that eventful period over a flowing bowl of whisky punch, while the report of their little noisy howitz awoke the echoes among the neighboring hills, at the announcement of each patriotic toast. A celebration of this glorious day without gunpowder or punch, would at that time have been called a burlesque.

"The last of February, 1795, about ten months after the massacre of Armstrong's family, Jonas Davis, a young man from Massachusetts, and an inmate of Stone's garrison, at the upper settlement, had been to Marietta, by land, and on his return, at the mouth of Crooked Creek, three miles from the Garrison, discovered an old skiff, or a small boat, that had been thrown on shore among some driftwood by the high water. Nails being scarce and dear at that time, he concluded to go up the next morning with some tools. pull it to pieces and get out the nails While busily occupied with the old skiff, a war party, consisting of two Indians and a negro who had been adopted by their

tribe, happened to be in that vicinity looking for an opportunity to kill or plunder the whites, heard him at work, and creeping up carefully to the edge of the bank, shot him, without his being aware of their approach; as was afterwards ascertained from one of the party, at the treaty of Greenville, in August following, where many things were disclosed in relation to the depredations on the settlements, that could only be learned from the Indians themselves. He was scalped, stripped of his clothing, his tools taken away, and his dead body left by the side of the skiff. As he did not return that night. fears were entertained of his fate, and the next morning a party of armed men went up, under the guidance of one of the rangers, where they found Davis as above related. He was brought down to the garrison and buried.

"His death was the most distressing as he was shortly to have been married to a daughter of Isaac Barker, one of the inhabitants of the garrison, and his wedding suit already prepared. Had he followed the rules of the station, which strictly forbade anyone going out alone beyond gunshot of the block-house, he would have escaped his untimely fate. The victory over the Indians by Wayne, and their quiet demeanor, since, no doubt induced him to think there was little or no danger. But as no treaty was yet concluded with the Indians. strict discipline was kept up in all the garrisons after that period, and no trust placed in their forbearance; for, although greatly humbled, their hatred of the whites was not lessened by their defeat.

"The day of the death of Davis, a party of four young men, headed by John James, Jr., one of the most active and resolute of the borderers, proceeded down the Ohio, in a canoe, in pursuit of the murders of Davis. The rangers at Gallipolis had ascertained

that a party of Indians were hunting on the head of Symmes' creek, and from the direction pursued by the war party in their retreat, they were led to think they belonged to that band. With all diligence they hastened on to the mouth of the Big Kanawha, in expectation of being joined there by volunteers from the garrison; but none turned out, declining to do so on account of the armistice made with the Indians after their defeat by General Wayne. Proceeding on to Gallipolis, and making known the object of their pursuit,, four men volunteered their aid and joined them. From this place they hastened onward to Raccoon Creek, and ranged up that stream one day without making any discovery of the Indians. Here one of their men fell sick and turned back, while another had to accompany him, leaving only six to continue. the pursuit.

"The following day they reached the head of Symmes' creek, where is a large pond, about a mile and a quarter of a mile wide, a famous place for trapping beaver. They soon fell upon signs of the Indians, and on a bush by the edge of the pond found an Indian's cap made of beaver skin, which he had left to mark the spot where his trap was set. Mr. James took this into his own keeping. As it was near sunset, the party secreted themselves behind a large fallen tree, waiting for night, when they intended to attack the Indians in their camp, make one fire and rush on with their tomahawks, not thinking the hunting party could number more than eight or ten men, but they subsequently found they amounted to near forty, divided into two camps, one on each side of the pond. They had lain concealed but a short time, when an Indian, who had been out hunting came in sight, and was closely examining the trail made by the whites,

knowing it was that of strangers. When he came within forty or fifty yards, one of the party, Joseph Miller, fired and the Indian fell. As Mr. James rushed up with his tomahawk he raised the war cry, and was instantly answered by his comrades in camp, distant not more than two or three hundred yards, for they came directly rushing up in force, before James could accomplish his purpose. and his party was obliged to retreat, as the Indians far outnumbered them. Seeing the whites likely to escape, they set their dogs on the trail, who came yelping and barking at their heels, like hounds in pursuit of a fox.

"Fortunately it soon came on so dark that their enemies could not see their trail, and followed only by the barking of the dogs. For a day or two previous it had rained heavily, and when they reached the east fork of the creek, it was too high for fording. They hastily made a raft of dry logs, but it became entangled in the bushes, in the creek bottom, which was all overflowed, so that they had to abandon it. Their escape this way being cut off, they were forced to return to the ridge, between the two branches, and travel up until they could cross by fording. A little before morning they halted and rested until daylight, the dogs for some time having ceased to pursue them, or by barking give notice of their position. Soon after this they found a fordable place in the creek and crossed over. Here they lay, an hour or two, waiting for the Indians, expecting them to pursue the trail with daylight and intending to fire upon them when in the water; but they did not come, having probably crossed higher up in the stream. When they reached Raccoon Creek, that was also full, and had to be crossed on a raft. The party reached Gallipolis the next day at evening, much wearied with their toilsome and exciting journey.

"Colonel Robert Safford of Gallipolis, then acting as a ranger, went out the next morning and found the trail of the Indians pursuing the whites to within a short distance of the town. The pond on Symmes' creek is distant about one hundred miles from Belpre, and shows this to have been one of the most hazardous, daring, and long-continued pursuits, after a depredating band of Indians, which occurred during the war, reflecting great credit on the spirited men who conducted it. It was the last warfare with the savages from this part of the territory.

"When at last the Indian war was ended, the families who had been so long and intimately associated together in Farmers' Castle, left their historic garrison to make once more homes for themselves in the land now forever reclaimed from the savages.

"Near the site of Farmers' Castle is the thriving village of Belpre, and just across the river lies the prosperous city of Parkersburg; tributes to the thrift and energy of this band of New England Pilgrims. Between the two towns lies the beautiful and historic island made famous by the names of Aaron Burr and Harman Blennerhassett.

"Previous to its occupancy by the latter, it was divided into farms which were occupied by early settlers. One of these was Captain James, who, with his family, from which, alas! one member was missing, removed to Blennerhasset Island, where they lived for several years.

"About 1798, he purchased a tract of land in West Virginia, seven hundred acres in extent, at the junction of Stillwell Creek, and the little Kanawha river, six miles from Parkersburg.

"Captain James, however, lived only a short time after removing his family to their new home, his death

occurring at the close of the eighteenth century, the latter part of which had proved so eventful for him and for his family, both in New England and in the 'Old Northwest.'

"The writer recently visited the site of the old home in West Virginia, which was afterward burned, and has in her possession an old English teaspoon upon which are inscribed the initials W. H., and which was thrown up by the plough a few years since, where once stood the home of Captain James.

"Of the seven hundred acres of land only a portion remains in the possession of his descendants; and upon this stands a substantial frame house, erected seventy-five years ago by his grandson, and still in a good state of preservation.

"Here in this peaceful spot, quiet, save for the occasional passing of a railway train, where the waters of Stillwell creek flow unceasingly into the Little Kanawha, and the hills encircle them with their protecting care, lie all that is mortal of Captain John James, and his wife, Esther Denison, who journeyed so long ago, from a comfortable home in New England, to endure the hardships of pioneer life in Ohio, and assist in founding the 'Empire of the West.'"

In 1906 a bronze tablet presented by the "Ohio Company of Associates of New York commemorating the first permanent settlement of the Ohio company, was unveiled on the Marietta college campus.

In July, 1908, the James Wood chapter, D. A. R., of Parkersburg, W. Va., dedicated a boulder to the memory of the revolutionary soldiers who are buried in Wood county, West Virginia. Among the names upon the bronze tablet is that of John James.

The year 1910 saw the erection and dedication by the Belpre Historical Society, of a monument which marks the site of Farmers' Castle.

A movement is in progress to organize in Jackson county, Ohio, a chapter of Daughters of the American Revolution which will bear the name of Captain John James, and still further preserve and honor the memory of a man, who, by his service to his country, and by a long and useful life, is entitled to the respect and veneration of his descendants.

One James Coat of Arms is as follows:

Arms—Azure, on a chevron between three lions passant gardant, or, as many escallops sable. Crest— A demi-lion rampant or holding an escallop sable.

The escallop shell was an emblem of the Pilgrim which he wore attached to his hat on his journeys to the Holy Land.

The motto of one James family of Wales is "Duw a Digon—God and enough"

As we do not know to what coat of arms our John James is entitled, none is given.

GENEALOGY.

Generations I and II.

John James (Gen. I, No. 1), b. probably at Exeter, Rhode Island; d. about 1799, near Parkersburg, West Virginia.; m. April 26, 1763, at Stonington, Conn., to Esther Denison, b. April 23, 1746, at Stonington, Conn.; d. after 1785, near Parkersburg, W Va. Residence: Exeter, R. I.; Preston, Conn ; Belpre, O., and Wood county, W. Va.

Authority for marriage record and line of descent: "Descendants of Captain George Denison," (Baldwin and Clift.)

Services: "A list of men who marched from Connecticut towns for the relief of Boston at the Lexington alarm: Corporal John James from the town of Preston." (Record of "Services of Connecticut men in the War of the Revolution " p. 20.)

"Muster roll of the company raised for the defense and protection of New London by Captain Mott in 1775, John James, sergeant." (Register of the Connecticut line. p. 617.)

"John James, of Preston, (also gives Stonington) as sergeant in Captain Peter's company, Colonel Timothy Danielson's regiment, with the eight months' army at the siege of Boston, 1775. The term of service expired December 31, 1775." (From "Soldiers and Sailors in the War of the Revolution," Vol. 8, Mass.)

"John James in Captain Barker's company, 5th regiment, February 23, 1778 " (See "Records of Conneticut Men, War of the Revolution," compiled by authority of the general assembly, Hartford, 1889.)

Captain James was a member of the "Ohio Company" which was formed at the close of the revolutionary war and came to Ohio in 1789.

Generation II.

Children of John and Esther (Denison) James.

2 Susannah, b. October, 1764.

3 Anna, b. July 28, 1766

4 William, b. May 18, 1769.

5 John, b. June 14, 1771.

6 Hannah, b. December 8, 1773.

7 Esther, b. September 22, 1775, d. January 23, 1776.

8 Abigail, b. March 17, 1777.

9 Polly, b. July 28, 1779.

10 Thomas, b. March 11, 1781.

11 Esther, b. January 3, 1783.

12 Simeon, b. April 29, 1785.

CHAPTER II.
Generations II and III.

Descendants of:

John (Gen. I, No. 1), and **Esther (Denison) James.**

Authority: Family records contributed by descendants.

Susannah James (Gen. II, No. 2), d. unm., and is buried at Warren, O.

Anna James (Gen. II, No. 3), b. July 28, 1766, at Preston, Conn.; d. probably at Parkersburg, W. Va ; m. Caleb Bailey.

Caleb Bailey was a merchant of Parkersburg, W. Va., in early days. More than a century ago he made a visit to England and while there purchased three silk dresses. One was a sky blue brocade, which he presented to his fiancee, Anna James. A green brocade was given to her sister, Hannah (James) Cook, and the third one, of black, to Polly, wife of Seth Bailey.

Anna wore hers as a wedding gown, and sixty years later, it was again used for the same purpose by her granddaughter, Emma Humphrey.

Generation III.

Children of Caleb and Anna (James) Bailey.

13 Charles P.
14 John A.
15 Sallie. —
16 Emma. ‿
17 Nancy.
18 Polly.

William James (Gen. II, No. 4), b. May 18, 1769,

at Preston, Conn., lost his life in Indian Massacre at "Big Bottom," January, 1791.

Hon. John James (Gen. II, No. 5), b. June 14, 1771, at Preston, Conn., d. May 31, 1854, at Jackson, O.; m. February 16, 1798, to Nancy Cook, b. June 15, 1775, at Long Plain, Mass., d. May 31, 1849, at Jackson, O.; (daughter of Captain Joseph Cook, Jr.) Residence, Jackson, O.

At the age of sixteen, John James lived for a time at Reading, Pa., but came to Ohio with his family a year or two later. He served in the Indian wars, gaining considerable prominence. From 1795 to 1800 he lived at Blennerhassett Island, W. Va.; afterward on James Island, now known as Neales Island.

He removed from there in 1806 to what is now Jackson, O., but was then only a salt works in the wilderness.

John James was six feet two inches in height, and weighed 220 pounds; was a successful business man, and a prominent member of the Methodist Episcopal church. He served in the war of 1812 under General Roop, and was afterward a member of the Ohio senate.

OBITUARY.

Died: At the residence of Daniel Hoffman, in the town of Jackson, on Wednesday, May 31, 1854, the Hon. John James.

The deceased was born in New London county, Connecticut, June 14, 1771, and emigrated to this state and landed at Fort Harmar in 1788. His father and family came the following year and settled on James' Island, about two miles above Parkersburg, W. Va. .

During his residence at Harmar and at Parkers-. burg, W. Va., his name is intimately associated with

the pioneers of that day in the trials, difficulties, sufferings and danger of a pioneer life, and at all times when necessary, he was an active and vigilant spy against the Indians, and in that capacity he traversed most of the counties of southern Ohio and western Virginia. In 1790 he visited the Spanish settlements on the Mississippi as a trader, his goods were seized and confiscated by the authorities, and he and his companions were compelled to travel on foot from Kaskaskia to Parkersburg, through a wilderness country inhabited only by tribes of Indians, then at war with our people.

On his return, he organized a second expedition for the same purpose, and in crossing the falls of the Ohio, one of his boats was sunk and those on board perished.

On the 16th of February, 1798, he married Nancy Cooke, a daughter of Joseph Cooke, of Parkersburg, W. Va. She died May 31, 1849.

In 1807, he came to this county, where he resided until his death, during which time he was elected to the senate and the house of representatives in the state of Ohio, and associate judge of Jackson county.

The deceased was a member of the Methodist church over forty years, and was a zealous and enthusiastic supporter of the religion of our Lord Jesus Christ, and in his last sickness, during which he suffered much and long (being confined several months) his confidence in the Savior appeared to grow stronger as he came near his time of departure, and but a few hours before his death, he sang with all his usual warmth his favorite hymn:

> "A charge to keep I have,
>   A God to glorify;
> A never dying soul to save,
>   And fit it for the sky."

He had a large stalwart frame; kind and benevolent face; was an affectionate husband and father; a sincere christian, benevolent to the poor, and a true hearted friend.

He lies buried in the Jamestown cemetery which derives its name from Major John James, on whose land it was laid out; his grave being on the Indian mound in the cemetery.

In the death of Mr. James, one of the old landmarks disappears. The name of James has been associated prominently with the entire history of Jackson; and "Jamestown" of itself, has come to be quite an important part of the place. The James are of good stock, and the family record holds an important place in the pioneer history of Ohio and the west."

Generation III.

Children of John and Nancy (Cook) James:

19 Nancy, b. November 22, 1798.
20 Julia, b. April 10, 1800.
21 Elizabeth, b. March 7, 1802.
22 Roanna, b. February 4, 1804.
23 John D., b. March 23, 1806.
24 William, b. March 23, 1806, d. August 28, 1806.
25 Harmeon, b. September 29, 1808.
26 Eliza, b. December 13, 1810.

Hannah James (Gen. II, No. 6), b. December 8, 1773, at Preston, Conn., d. May 12, 1843, at Parkersburg, W. Va.; (Buried in the old Cook burying ground). m. (1) to Benjamin Johnson, (2) to Bennett Cook, (a brother of Nancy (Cook) James), b. October 3, 1776, at Long Plain, Mass.; d. October 9, 1845, at Parkersburg, W. Va. Residence, Parkersburg. W. Va.

Bennett Cook was the third child of Capt. Joseph Cook, Jr., and went to sea while yet a boy, and was absent in Europe when his parents removed to the west. Upon his return he joined them accompanied by his uncle, Pardon Cook. He purchased a farm of one hundred acres and built the large brick dwelling house still standing (January 1, 1907.)

He was appointed justice of the peace for Wood county, Virginia, and in 1826 and 1827 became ex-officio high sheriff of the same county. He became, later in life, presiding justice of the county court.

Generation III.

Children of Bennett and Hannah (Johnson) Cook.

27 Harriet, b, July 17, 1807; d October 30, 1820.

28 Paul, b. October 2, 1809.

29 James, b. October, 1810, d. 1811.

30 Bennett, b. February 8, 1812.

31 John James, b. January 18, 1814.

Abigail James (Gen. II, No. 8), b. March 17, 1777, at Preston, Conn, d. June 15, 1832, in Jackson county, Ohio; m. March 26, 1801, in Wood county, West Virginia, to David Paine, b. September 14, 1775, in Hampshire county, Massachusetts, d. January 5, 1856, in Jackson county, Ohio. (See Paine family No. 108.)

Authority for marriage record: Certified copy of marriage record from office of clerk of Wood county, West Virginia. Residence, Preston, Conn., Wood county, West Virginia,; Jackson county, Ohio.

Generation III.

Children of David and Abigail (James) Paine.

Authority for line of descent: Family Bible of Judge David Paine, now in possession of Mrs. J. B. Foraker.

32 Eliza, b. March 13, 1802; d. March, 1804.
33 David, b. October 7, 1804; d. 1805.
34 Melissa, b. October 24, 1805.
35 Lemuel Shepherd. b. August 15, 1807.
36 Thomas Denison, b. September 27, 1810.
37 Sarah, b. May 31, 1813
38 Johnathan Douglas. b. September 8, 1815.
39 Caroline, b. May 25, 1817.

Polly James (Gen. II, No. 9), b July 28, 1779, at Stonington, Conn, d. September 4. 1852, at Warren, O.; m. 1800, to Seth Bailey, Jr., b. June 1, 1778, at Easton, Mass. d. March 7, 1861, at Warren, O.; (son of Seth and Deborah (Packard) Bailey.)

Authority· Family record compiled by Ellen Frances Bailey (No. 188.) Residence, Warren, O.; (now Constitution, O.)

"Polly (James) Bailey was a woman of great force of character and at one time was the only professing christian in the township. She was one of the constituent members of the Warren Presbyterian church.

During the sickly season of 1822-23, when almost every family for miles around, lost one or more members, they carried their large family of eleven children through without the loss of one, and without the aid of a physician. Beside their own large family they brought up five nieces and nephews, and another little girl who was left an orphan.

. Seth Bailey, a native of Massachusetts, emigrated to Virginia in 1798 While there he married Polly, the daughter of Captain John James, who at that time owned Vienna Island, Neals Island and a large tract of land in Virginia.

Polly received as a marriage portion Vienna Island. Mr. Bailey built a cabin on the island and began the work of clearing in 1802.

He at this time owned one horse, two oxen and one cow. The island was densely covered with immense trees, and clearing progressed slowly and involved the hardest kind of labor.

Winter set in before a shelter could be provided for the stock, but nature had supplied that. A sycamore tree, seventeen feet in its greatest diameter, and fifteen in its shortest, was discovered to be hollow. A door was cut in one side and the interior found large enough to afford a comfortable shelter for all the stock. In after years the tree caught fire and burned to the ground.

Mr. Bailey one year later planted corn inside the remaining snags and harvested from it one bushel.

Early in 1805, a frame house was built opposite the head of the island. This house became the Bailey homestead (From history of Washington county, Ohio, page 635.)

Seth Bailey was one of the pioneer settlers of Ohio. At the time of his death, he was one of the most venerable, as he was one of the most respected and esteemed of the citizens of Washington county.

Having secured for himself a sufficient estate, he spent his last years in freedom from care, and exhibited a rare instance of a genial and hearty old age. He was a lover of education and good morals: and was for many years a member of the Presbyterian church.'' (Bailey Genealogy.)

Generation III.

Children of Seth and Polly (James) Bailey.

40 Maria, b. April 6, 1803.

41 Elizabeth, b. September, 1804, d. unm. January 10, 1872.

42 Seth, b. September 9, 1806.

43 Charles Pease, b. 1808.

44 John James, b. April 15, 1810.

45 Susan Uhl, b. 1811

46 Bennett Cook, b. November 28, 1813.

47 William Denison. b. May 24, 1816.

48 George Washington, b. December 12, 1817.

49 Augustus Stone, b. 1819.

50 Thomas James, b. April 22, 1822, d unm. in 1882.

Esther James (Gen. II, No. 11), b. January 3, 1783, at Preston, Conn., m. ———— Gillespie and removed to the west.

CHAPTER III.

Generations III and IV.

Descendants of:

Caleb and Anna (James) Bailey (Gen. II, No. 3)
Authority· Family record compiled by descendants.

Charles P. Bailey (Gen. III, No. 13), b. probably
at Parkersburg, W. Va, m. Elizabeth Harwood.
Residence, Wood County, West Virginia.

Generation IV.

Children of Charles P. and Elizabeth (Harwood) Bailey.

51 Gassaway.
52 Nancy.
53 Charles.
54 Henry.
55 Elizabeth.
56 James.

John A. Bailey (Gen. III, No. 14), b. at Parkersburg, W. Va., m. ————.

Generation IV.

Children of John A. and ———— Bailey.

57 Kitty, m. Whitten Dole, lives in Maine.

Descendants of:

Hon. John (Gen. II, No. 5) and Nancy (Cook)
James.

Authority: Family record contributed by Julia
Johnson, No. 89, and Ada M. Ervin, No. 337.

Nancy James (Gen. III, No. 19), b. November 22, 1798, on Blennerhassett Island, m. July 29, 1819, to Cornelius Millar.

Residence, Jackson county, Ohio.

Generation IV.

Children of Cornelius and Nancy (James) Millar.

58 Jane.
59 Julia Ann, b. 1826.
60 Rebecca, b 1831.
61 Cornelius Elton, b. January 4, 1833.

Julia James (Gen. III, No. 20), b April 10, 1800, on James Island, Ohio river. d. June 16, 1863, at Jackson, O ; m. August 28, 1818, at Jackson, O., to Daniel Hoffman, b January 18, 1790, d. August 28, 1861.

Residence, Jackson, O.

Authority: Family records contributed by D. A. Hoffman, No. 64.

Julia (James) Hoffman was the mother of five sons and one daughter, all of whom were liberally educated—the sons professionally.

She joined the M. E church at the age of fourteen and remained a faithful member until the separation of the M. P. from the M. E. church, when she became identified with the former. Her later years were filled with great suffering, but marked also by much patience and resignation.

Daniel Hoffman was a prominent man and a merchant.

Generation IV.

Children of Daniel and Julia (James) Hoffman.

62 John James, b. May 7, 1825.

63 Ripley Christian, b. September 25, 1822.

64 David Allen, b. September 28, 1824.

65 Charles Bardwell, b. 1826, d. at six months.

66 Cornelia Virginia, b. April 21, 1836.

67 Daniel Webster, b November 12, 1840

Elizabeth James (Gen. III, No. 21), b. March 7, 1802, on James Island, Ohio river, d. 1872; m. December 9, 1818, to Hooper Hurst, b. 1793, d. 1848.

Residence, Jackson county, Ohio, and Ross County, Ohio.

Authority Family records contributed by Elizabeth (Paine) Cherrington, No. 245.

Generation IV.

Children of Hooper and Elizabeth (James) Hurst.

68 Julia Ann, b. October 1819.

69 Nancy, b. 1823

70 Levi James, b. 1825.

71 John Rathburn, b 1827.

72 Denison, b. 1829.

73 Samuel H , b 1831.

74 William Fletcher, b 1833.

75 Louisa Hermione, b. 1838.

76 Emily Lucretia, b. 1843.

77 Elizabeth Cecilia, b. 1845.

Roanna James (Gen. III, No. 22), b. February 4, 1804, on James Island, Ohio river, d. October 17. 1891, at Jackson, O , m. (1) July 24, 1821, at Jackson, O., to Dr. John W. Rathburn; m. (2) November 13, 1834, at Jackson, O., to Dr. Elihu Johnson, b. June 28, 1793, in Iredell county, North Carolina, d. December 20, 1886, at Jackson, O.

Authority: Family records contributed by Julia Johnson, No. 89.

Generation IV.

Children of John W. and Roanna (James) Rathburn.

78 Harriet, b May 3, 1822.
79 John, b. October 30, 1823.
80 Joseph.
81 Romaine, b. May 9, 1827.
82 Charles, b. 1829.
83 Eliza

Generation IV.

Children of Elihu and Roanna (Rathburn) Johnson.

84 George W., b. August 7, 1835.
85 Adelia, b. 1837, d unm. 1854.
86 Pauline, b. March 17, 1839.
87 Lucretia, b October 15, 1842.
88 Leonidas, b. 1845, unm.
89 Julia, b. January 21, 1848.

John Denison James (Gen. III, No. 23), b. March 23, 1806, on James Island, Ohio river, d. September 4, 1887, at Jamestown, near Jackson, O.; m. July 26, 1832, at Jackson, O , to Sarah Mitchell, daughter of Hon. David Mitchell.

Residence, Jackson county, Ohio.

Authority: Family records contributed by Adeline M. Ervin, No. 337.

OBITUARY OF JOHN DENISON JAMES.

At his residence in Jamestown, near Jackson, O., on Sabbath, 12 o'clock, September 4, ——, John Denison James, aged 81 years, 5 months and 12 days.

He was born on James Island in the Ohio river, about two miles above Parkersburg, W. Va., March 23, 1806, but since 1807 has lived in Jackson, O.

He was fifth of the family of Hon. John James, one of the first settlers of Jackson county. He lived to see the country grow from a dense forest to a populated and well improved country which he was in part instrumental in bringing about.

In 1832 he married Sarah, daughter of Hon David Mitchell, by whom he had thirteen children. He joined the M. E church in his twenty-first year and remained a faithful and acceptable member until the separation of the M. P. from the M. E. church.

For many years his home was known as the "Preachers' Home" where servants of God were welcomed and refreshed. During his entire life he maintaind a character of the most unblemished and practical christianity and unbending integrity. Ever cheerful and kind was his greeting to the aged and young and many there are who will miss the cheery smiling face of "Uncle Denison."

Generation IV.

Children of John D. and Sarah (Mitchell) James.

.   90 Matiller, b. January 3, 1834, d. October 22, 1834.

91 John Ripley, b. August 9, 1835.

92 David M., b. May 25, 1837.

93 Thomas Denison, b. March 3, 1839.

94 Nancy Cook, b. October 3, 1840.

95 Charles Curtland, b. December 29, 1842.

96 Zachariah Ragon, b. October 16, 1844.

97 Mary Eleanor, b. October 19, 1846.

98 Edward Mitchell, b. June 4, 1848.

99 Eliza Elizabeth, b. March 19, 1850.

100 Franklin, b January 29, 1852.

101 Tryphena, b. September 20, 1854.

102 Ida May, b. May 20, 1858.

Harmeon James (Gen. III, No. 25), b. September 29, 1808, at Jackson, O., d. July 31, 1886, at Jackson, O.; m. August 21, 1825, at Jackson, O., to Alexander Miller, b. December 15, 1794, d. March 19, 1853.

Authority: Family records contributed by Mary May Miller, No. 327.

Harmeon James was a member of the Methodist Protestant church. She was an invalid for many years but a busy woman withal, and her acts of kindness, her happy disposition, and inborn characteristic James wit, with her kind motherly heart, endeared her to all who knew her. She spent the last years of her life in the home of her son Alonzo and is buried in the Jamestown cemetery, just south of the Indian mound.

Generation IV.

Children of Alexander and Harmeon (James) Miller.

103 Mary E., b. August 26, 1826.
104 Emily, b. May 6, 1828.
105 Barbara, b March 16, 1830, d. August, 11, 1834.
106 Edward, b. April 17, 1833, d. July 18, 1834.
107 David Allen, b. April 25, 1835.
108 Maria, b. July 10, 1837.
109 Alonzo, b. January 14, 1844.
110 Addie, b. August 1, 1850.

Eliza James (Gen. III, No. 26,) b. December 13, 1810, in Jackson county, Ohio, d. July 26, 1874, at Jackson, O.; m. September 1, 1831, at Jackson, O., to Andrew Long, b. July 24, 1810, in Virginia, d. 1869, at Jackson, O.

Residence, Jackson, O.

Like her sisters, Eliza (James) Long, familiarly known as "Aunt Eliza" Long, was a devout christian and one of the earliest members of the M. E. church in Jackson.

Blest with the "good things of life" she found many opportunities for christian work, and how well she employed these with her hands, her prayers and her means, has become a matter of history. Naturally timid and reserved yet she possessed keen penetration.

The air of triumph with which she met death after months of intense suffering will never be forgotten by those who knew her. Her favorite expression was "Peace, peace, all peace, not a doubt, not a cloud, perfect peace."

Generation IV.

Children of Andrew and Eliza (James) Long.

111 Amanda, b. August 28, 1832.
112 Elias, b. November 30, 1835.
113 John James, b. February 13, 1842.
114 Jacob A., b. February 24, 1847.

Descendants of:

Bennett and Hannah (Johnson) Cook (Gen. II, No. 6.)

Authority: Family records contributed by Clara (Cook) McCluer, No. 131.

Paul Cooke (Gen. III, No. 28), b. October 2, 1809, ·in Wood county West Virginia, d. May 28, 1881, near Parkersburg, W. Va.; m. December 31, 1831, to Julia A. Kincheloe, d November 1, 1869, near Parkersburg, W. Va.; daughter of Jeptha Kincheloe.

Residence, Worthington Creek, W. Va.

Generation IV.

Children of Paul and Julia (Kincheloe) Cooke.

115 Harriet, b. January 6. 1833.
116 Sarah, b. November 14, 1834.

117 Maria, b. November 11, 1836.

118 Henry C., b. May 11, 1839.

119 Mary F., b. October 31, 1841.

120 Hannah, b. November 8, 1843.

121 Laura, b. January 15, 1853.

Bennett Cooke (Gen III, No. 30), b. February 8, 1812, in Wood county, West Virginia, d. September 23, 1883, near Parkersburg, W. Va.; m. August 26, 1841, probably at Union, O., to Julia Maria Devol, b. March 29, 1819, d May 5, 1893, daughter of Francis Devol, of Union, O.

Residence, Parkersburg, W. Va.

Generation IV.

Children of Bennett and Julia (Devol) Cooke.

122 Frances V., b. September 4, 1843.

123 Bennett, b. July 10, 1846, d. July 19, 1902.

124 Letha Devol, b. March 10, 1848.

125 Charles Hildreth, b. June 6, 1850, d. September 6, 1852.

Hon. John James Cooke (Gen. III, No. 31), b. January 18, 1814, in Wood county, West Virginia, d. May 4, 1870, probably at Parkersburg, W. Va.; m. January 2, 1840, probably in Wood county, West Virginia, to Sophia K. Kincheloe, b. April 2, 1815, d. May 26, 1886; daughter of Jeptha Kincheloe, of Wood county West Virginia

Residence, Parkersburg, W. Va.

Hon. John James Cooke was a member of the house of delegates of Virginia, 1849-50; acting sheriff of Wood county for many years; president of the Northwestern Virginia Railway Company, 1851-52; president of the Northwestern Bank of Virginia at Parkersburg, and president of the council of the corporation of Parkersburg.

Generation IV.

Children of John James and Sophia (Kincheloe) Cooke.

126 Jeptha Kincheloe, b. October 6, 1840, d. September 20, 1850.

127 Bennett, b. October 9, 1843, d. June 25, 1845.

128 Fanny M., b. July 21, 1846.

129 Laura, b. September 9, 1848, d. August 29, 1852.

130 Sophia, b. 1852, d. 1869.

131 Clara Bettie, b. January 29, 1854.

132 Mary James, b. April 6, 1856, d. September 21, 1906.

133 Julia, b. April 27, 1863.

Descendants of:

David and Abigail (James) Paine (Gen. II, No. 8.)

Melissa Paine (Gen III, No. 34), b. October 24, 1805, in Wood county, West Virginia, d. 1879, at Wilkesville, O.; m. January 20, 1831, in Jackson county, Ohio, to Jacob W. Hawk, b. January 30, 1807, d. February 9, 1883, at Wilkesville, O.

Authority: Family records contributed by Amanda Hawk, No. 136.

Generation IV.

Children of Jacob and Melissa (Paine) Hawk.

134 Francis Asberry, b. December 25, 1831.

135 Melissa Abigail, b. March 5, 1834.

136 Amanda Eleanor, b. August 2, 1836.

137 James Monroe, b. July 4, 1840.

138 Caroline Paine, b. June 27, 1842.

139 Mary E., b. October 3, 1844

140 Eliza Ophelia, b. February 21, 1847.

141 David Wilmot, b. June 2, 1850.

Lemuel Shepherd Paine (Gen. III, No. 35), b. August 15, 1807, in Wood county, West Virginia, d. March 25, 1878, at Hamden, O., m. September 1, 1842, at Tarlton, O, to Elizabeth Roby, b. May 16, 1820, at Tarlton, O., d. January 29, 1890, at Lima, O.

Residence, Hamden, O.

Authority: Family records contributed by Clara P. Ohler, No. 148.

Generation IV.

Children of Lemuel S. and Elizabeth (Roby) Paine.

142 Mary Caroline, b. August 27, 1843, d. September 2, 1843.

    143 James Basil, b. October 1, 1844.

    144 David Sanford, b. August 23, 1846.

    145 Bennett Roby, b. August 27, 1848.

    146 Delia Elizabeth, b March 4, 1851.

    147 William Denison, b. October 7, 1860.

    148 Clara May, b. July 24, 1862.

Sarah Paine (Gen. III, No. 37), b. May 31, 1813, in Jackson county, Ohio, d August 2, 1886, in Ross county, Ohio; m. October 11, 1832, in Jackson county, Ohio, to John Nelson Hurst, b January 6, 1808, at Chillicothe, O., d. August 12, 1889, in Ross county O.

Authority: Family records contributed by J. M. Hurst, No. 153.

Generation IV.

Children of John N. and Sarah (Paine) Hurst.

    149 David L., b. July 8, 1834.

    150 Eliza, b. March 25, 1836.

    151 Wilson R., b. December 23, 1837.

    152 Caroline L., b. March 24, 1839.

    153 Joseph M., b. February 7, 1841.

154 Amanda, b. November 19, 1843.
155 Douglas T., b. October 2, 1846.
156 Charles B. b. May 11, 1852.

Jonathan Douglas Paine (Gen. III, No. 38), b. September 8, 1815, in Jackson county, Ohio, d. June 12, 1846, in Jackson county, Ohio; m. May, 1839, in Ross county, Ohio, to Julia Ann Hurst, b. October 18, 1819, in Jackson county, Ohio, d. November 17, 1898, at Columbus, O.

Authority· Family records contributed by Elizabeth (Paine) Cherrington, No. 157.

Generation IV.

Children of Jonathan D and Julia (Hurst) Paine.

157 Elizabeth Ophelia, b. August 3, 1841.

Caroline Paine (Gen. III, No. 39), b. May 25, 1817, in Jackson, county, Ohio, d. January 4, 1868, in Jackson county, Ohio; m. March 28, 1844, in Jackson county, Ohio, to Hezekiah Sanford Bundy, b. August 15, 1817, at Marietta, O., d. December 12, 1895, at Wellston, O.

Authority: Family records contributed by Julia (Bundy) Foraker, No. 159.

Generation IV.

Children of Hezekiah and Caroline (Paine) Bundy.

158 David Denison, b. March 14, 1845, d. 1846.
159 Julia Ann Paine, b. June 17, 1847.
160 Eliza Melinda, b. June 17, 1850.

- Descendants of:

Seth and Polly (James) Bailey (Gen. II, No. 9.)
Authority: Family records contributed by Ellen Frances Bailey, No. 190.

Maria Bailey (Gen. III, No. 40), b. April 6, 1803, on Vienna (or James) Island, d September 16, 1889, at Elmdale, Kan.; m. March 18, 1830, to Frederic Shipman, b. August 30, 1795, at Marietta, O., d August 26, 1889, at Marietta, O.; son of Joshua and Sibyl Shipman.

Residence, Marietta, O.

Generation IV.

Children of Frederic and Maria (Bailey) Shipman.

161 Mary Sibyl, b. December 28, 1830.
162 Joshua Seth, b. March 6, 1832.
163 Julia Maria, b. February 23, 1835.
164 Charles F., b. 1838, d. 1844.

Seth Bailey (Gen III, No. 42), b. September 9, 1806, at Warren, O., d May 27, 1884, at Coolville, O.; m. (1) December 31, 1833, to Sarah Devol McClure, b. September 30, 1809, in Washington county, Ohio, daughter of Andrew and Mary (Devol) McClure; m. (2) September 17, 1839, near Wheeling, W. Va., to Mary Ann Scott, b. April 19, 1814, d. February 3, 1907, daughter of John and Nancy Scott.

Generation IV.

Children of Seth and Sarah (McClure) Bailey.
165 Mary.

Generation IV.

Children of Seth and Mary (Scott) Bailey.
166 Nancy Ann.
167 Isabella.
168 Lydia Jane.
169 Sarah Elizabeth, d. in infancy, June, 1849.

170 Seth Austin.
171 Julia Augusta.
172 Alice Rosetta.

Charles Pease Bailey (Gen. III, No. 43), b 1808, in Washington county, Ohio, d. 1879, in Virginia; m. 1837, to Harriett Chapman, daughter of Isaac and Sarah (Perkins) Chapman She m. (2) Mr Van Ness

John James Bailey (Gen. III, No. 44), b. April 15, 1810, d. May 9. 1849; m January 25, 1836, near Salem, O., to Mary Chapman, b. April 15, 1812, d. May 2, 1859, daughter of Isaac and Sarah (Perkins) Chapman. She m. (2) James Hunter.

Generation IV.

Children of John James and Mary (Chapman) Bailey.

173 Charles Chapman, b. November 6, 1836, d. January 13, 1841.

174 Sarah, b. July 8, 1838.

175 John Worthington.

176 Elizabeth Burgess, b. September 10, 1844, d. 1845.

177 Georgette Elizabeth, b. June 6, 1846, d. 1849.

Susan Uhl Bailey (Gen. III, No. 45), b. 1811, at Warren, O., d. 1853, at Warren, O ; m. 1841, to Dr. G. A. Ward, son of Dr. Walter Ward.

Generation IV.·

Children of G. A. and Susan (Bailey) Ward.

178 Frances Elizabeth.
179 George Rollin.
180 Orlando, d. young.
181 Mary Celeste.
182 Walter Payson.
183 Henry.

Bennett Cook Bailey (Gen III, No. 46), b. November 28, 1813, at Warren, O., d. 1890, at Newton, Kan.; m February 22. 1844, to Fannie Mary Dickey, b. February 8, 1818, in Washington county, Ohio, d. January 20, 1884, at Newton, Kan.

Residence, Warren, O., Newton, Kan.

Generation IV.

Children of Bennett and Fannie (Dickey) Bailey.

184 Mary Elizabeth, b. 1845, d. June 3, 1893.
185 James Dickey, b. 1846, d July 10, 1875.
186 Harriet Dickey.
. 187 Seth Packard.
188 Bennett Augustus.

William Denison Bailey (Gen. III. No. 47), b. May 24, 1816, at Constitution, O., d. April 10, 1894, at Marietta, O , m. (1) May 10, 1848, to Mary Annette Ward, b. April 25, 1822, d. April 25, 1849, daughter of Dr. Walter Ward; m. (2) October 1, 1850, to Elizabeth Smith Emerson, b. March 19, 1820, daughter of Caleb and Mary (Dana) Emerson.

Generation IV.

Children of William D. and Mary (Ward) Bailey.

189 Mary Annette.

Generation IV.

Children of William and Elizabeth (Emerson) Bailey.

190 Ellen Frances.
191 Lucy Denison.
192 William Emerson, d. young.
193 Charles Emerson.

George Washington Bailey (Gen III, No 48,) b. December 12, 1817, at Warren, O., d. December 26, 1903, m 1855 at Vienna, W. Va., to Sarah Jane Stapleton daughter of Joshua and Eliza Stapleton.

Generation IV.

Children of George W. and Sarah (Stapleton) Bailey.
194 Sarah Bertha.
195 Eliza Alberta.
196 Minnie Maud.
197 George Howard.

Augustus Stone Bailey (Gen. III, No. 49), b. November 19, 1819, at Warren, O, d. at Elmdale, Kan.; m. April 13, 1852, in Athens county, Ohio, to Julia Ann Johnson.

Residence, Warren, O.; after 1874, Elmdale, Kan.

Generation IV.

Children of Augustus and Julia (Johnson) Bailey.

198 Emma.

199 Clara Katherine.

CHAPTER IV.

Generation IV and V.

Descendants of:

Charles P. (Gen. III, No. 13), and **Elizabeth (Harwood) Bailey.**

Authority: Family records contributed by Laura (DeVaughan) Bailey.

Nancy Bailey (Gen. IV, No. 52), m. 1842, to Benjamin Butcher.

Residence, Wood county, West Virginia.

Generation V.

Children of Benjamin and Nancy (Bailey) Butcher.

200 Henry, b. 1843, m. Jane Deems.

201 Mary, b. 1845, m. Perry Lewis.

202 Henrietta, b 1847, m William Stout.

203 Charles, b. 1849.

204 Margaret.

205 Mildred.

206 James, m. Cora Lewis.

207 Frank, b 1857, m. Elizabeth Phillips.

208 Lucy, b. 1860, m. Andrew Clark Cook.

209 Josephine, b. 1863, m. Charles Robbins.

James Bailey (Gen. IV, No. 56), m. 1871 to Laura DeVaughan.

Residence, Wood county, West Virginia.

Generation V.

Children of James and Luara (DeVaughan) Bailey.

210 Charles P., b. 1873.

211 Bessie, b. December 4, 1875.

212 William B., b 1877.

213 Nancy, b 1879.

214 Warren C., b 1884. Member of signal corps
U. S. army.

Descendants of:

Cornelius and **Nancy (James) Millar** (Gen. III, No.
19.)

Authority Family records contributed by Mary
M. Miller, No. 327.

Jane Millar (Gen. IV, No. 58), b. in Jackson county, Ohio, d. at age of 78, m Sanford Williams.

Generation V.

Children of Sanford and Jane (Millar) Williams.

215 Rebecca.

216 Hannah.

Julia Ann Millar (Gen. IV, No. 59), b. 1826, d.
January, 1899; m. 1848 to J. L. Gibson. (Two children died in infancy.)

Rebecca Millar (Gen. IV, No. 60), b. 1831, d. 1892;
m. 1855 to Samuel Sargent.

Generation V.

Children of Samuel and Rebecca (Millar) Sargent

217 Algernon.

218 Minnie.

219 Julia.

220 Samuel.

Cornelius Elton Millar (Gen. IV, No 61), b. January 4, 1833, m. 1858 to Mary Chenoweth

Generation V.

Children of Cornelius and Mary (Chenoweth) Millar.

221 Austin.
222 Kate
223 Jessie.
224 William.
225 Franklin
226 Elton, Jr.
Descendants of:

Daniel and Julia (James) Hoffman (Gen. III, No. 20.)

Authority: Family records contributed by D. A. Hoffman, No 64.

Ripley Christian Hoffman (Gen. IV, No. 63), b. September 25, 1822, at Jackson, O., d. April 14, 1900, at Columbus, O.; m. October 5. 1843, at Athens, O., to Lucy Matilda Fuller, b. May 14, 1822, at Athens, O., d July 22, 1874. at Columbus, O., daughter of James and Mary (Walker) Fuller. m (2) December 21, 1875, at Columbus, O., to Mary Eliza Sullivant, b. July 7, 1844, at Columbus, O., d. March 17, 1905.

Residence, Columbus, O.

Generation V.

Children of Ripley C. and Lucy (Fuller) Hoffman.

227 James Fuller, b. August 12, 1844.
228 Daniel, b. January 22, 1848, d. unm. August 11, 1869.
229 Frank Ferno, b January 19, 1852, unm. attorney-at-law, lives at Columbus, O
230 Harry Brown, b. May 8, 1861, d. October 11, 1864.

Generation V.

Children of Ripley C. and Mary (Sullivant) Hoffman.

231 Arthur Sullivant b. September 28, 1876

David Allen Hoffman (Gen. IV, No 64), b. September 28, 1824 at Jackson. O.. d. at Oskaloosa, Ia., m. November 16. 1848. at Logan, O.. to Emily Smith, b. January 18, 1830

Residence. Oskaloosa. Ia.

Generation V.

Children of David and Emily (Smith) Hoffman.

232 Edgar Brown b. August 25, 1849
233 John Adams b. April 23. 1851.
234 Effie Louise. b. May 14, 1853.
235 Ripley Christian. b. November 12, 1860.

Cornelia Virginia Hoffman (Gen. IV, No. 66), b. April 21, 1836, at Jackson. O , d. May 31, 1893, at Jackson, O.; m. September 14, 1853, to John L. Long, b. February 18, 1825, at Jackson, O , d. July 21, 1898.

Residence, Jackson. O.

Generation V.

Children of John L. and Cornelia (Hoffman) Long.

236 Herbert, b. September 27, 1854, d. June 8, 1855.
237 Fanny, b February 5, 1859.
238 Grace Correll. b November 9, 1861.
239 Harry Hoffman. b. March 27, 1866.
240 Stella Marie, b September 1, 1868.
241 Cornelia Virginia. b. July 3, 1875.

Major Daniel Webster Hoffman (Gen. IV, No. 67), b. November 12, 1840, at Jackson, O., d. December 26, 1875, m December 20, 1866, to Lucy C. Gillett.

Generation V.

Children of Daniel and Lucy (Gillett) Hoffman.

242 Florence Delano, b. February 9, 1868, in Ottawa, Kan.

243 William Gillett, b. May 3, 1871, in Ottawa, Kan.

244 Douglas Ripley, b. November 30, 1874, at Circleville, O.

Descendants of:

Hooper and Elizabeth (James) Hurst (Gen. III, No. 21.)

Authority   Family records contributed by Elizabeth (Paine) Cherrington, No. 245.

Julia Ann Hurst (Gen. IV. No. 68), b. October, 1819, in Jackson county, Ohio, d. 1898, at Columbus, O.; m. (1) May. 1839, in Jackson county, Ohio, to Jonathan Douglas Paine, b. September 8, 1815, in Jackson county, Ohio. d. June 12, 1846, in Jackson county, Ohio; (see Paine family, chapter VII), m. (2) 1851, to Rev. William W. Cherrington, d. December 16, 1887.

Julia Ann Hurst was a woman noted for her good works and useful life, which was a sermon in itself.

Her children, all carefully educated, repaid her for her sacrifices and loving care which she gave them, and her good influence will be felt through generations to come. She united with the M E. church at the age of nine years, of which she was a devoted member during her life.

Nobly and faithfully she did her part as a minister's wife. In the inner court of her home, in the outer court of the world, in the holy places of the church, and in the holy of holies on high, it will be said of this faithful woman of God that "she hath done what she could."

Generation V.

Children ot Douglas and Julia (Hurst) Paine.

245 Elizabeth Ophelia, b. August 3, 1841.

Generation V.

Children of W. W. and Julia (Paine) Cherrington.

246 William Douglas, b. June 6, 1852.
247 Charles Simpson, b December 22, 1854.
248 Lemuel Bundy, b. June, 1857.
249 Edgar Hurst, b. January 23, 1860.
250 Lora Eleanor, b. April 27, 1862.

Nancy Hurst (Gen. IV, No. 69), b. 1823, d. 1900; m. Uriah Betts, b. 1825, d. 1893.
Residence, Clarksburg, O.

Generation V.

Children of Uriah and Nancy (Hurst) Betts.

251 Julia.
252 Laura.
253 Thomas.
254 Albert.

Levi James Hurst (Gen. IV, No. 70), b. 1825, d. 1898, m. Clara Dodge, b. 1833, d. 1886.

Generation V.

Children of Levi and Clara (Dodge) Hurst.

255 Flora, d. at the age of six.
256 Minnie, living in Iowa.
257 Mary, living in Iowa.

John Rathburn Hurst (Gen. IV, No. 71), b. 1827; m. in Ross county, Ohio, to Elizabeth Hawkins.

Generation V.

Children of John and Elizabeth (Hawkins) Hurst.

258 Eugene.
259 Clinton.

Denison Hurst (Gen. IV, No. 72), b. 1829, d. 1906; m Minerva Wilson, b. 1835, d. 1890.

General Samuel H. Hurst (Gen. IV, No. 73), b. September 22, 1831, in Ross county, Ohio, d July 27, 1908, at Chillicothe, O., m. (1) Mary Trimble, b. 1839, d. 1874; m. (2) Mrs. Fredrika Hawley.

Residence, Chillicothe, O.

General Hurst was a graduate of Ohio Wesleyan University in 1854; superintendent of schools at Jackson, O., 1854-55; admitted to the bar in 1858; elected city solicitor 1859; probate judge 1860. Captain of Company A. 73rd regiment, Ohio Volunteer Infantry promoted to the rank of major, June 1862; promoted to lieutenant colonel, 1864, colonel in June, 1864, commanding his regiment through the "Atlanta Campaign" and "Sherman's March to the Sea." In March, 1865, Colonel Hurst was brevetted brigadier general.

In 1869 he was appointed internal revenue collector for his congressional district.

Generation V.

Children of Samuel and Mary (Trimble) Hurst.

260 Maud, d. at age of sixteen.
261 Luther.
262 Madge.
263 Mary.

Generation V.

Children of Samuel and Fredrika (Hawley) Hurst.

264 Edith.

265 Carl.

William Fletcher Hurst (Gen IV, No. 74), b. 1833, d 1883; m. Mary Rockwell, b. 1838, d. 1904.

Generation V.

Children of William and Mary (Rockwell) Hurst.

266 Harry.

267 Charles.

268 Elizabeth.

269 William.

Louisa Hermione Hurst (Gen. IV, No. 75), b. 1838; m. John Abernathy, b. 1827, d 1899. No children.

Emily Lucretia Hurst (Gen. IV, No. 76), b. 1843, d. 1900; m. Robert Doyle, b. 1843.

Generation V.

Children of Robert and Emily (Hurst) Doyle.

270 Lucile, b. October 17, 1869.

271 John H., b. September 23, 1872.

272 Petra, b. May 10, 1877.

Elizabeth Cecelia Hurst (Gen. IV, No. 77), b. 1845; m. Dr. Daniel A. Hare, b. 1847, d. 1896.

Children of Daniel and Elizabeth (Hurst) Hare.

Generation V.

273 Ernest.

274 Blanche.

275 Claude.

Descendants of:

John W. and Roanna (James) Rathburn (Gen. III, No. 22.)

Authority: Family records contributed by Ada-lite M. Ervin, No. 337

Harriet Cooke Rathburn (Gen. IV, No. 78), b May 3, 1822, at Jackson, O , d. August 15, 1893, at Ashland, Neb : m. June 5, 1840, at Jackson, O., to Joseph Throckmorton. b. July 8, 1815 at Steubenville, O., d. December 18, 1888, at Ashland, Neb.

A quaint document dated December 5, 1864, is the license issued by the Nebraska conference to Joseph Throckmorton to "exhort."

Generation V.

Children of Joseph and Harriet (Rathburn) Throck-morton.

276 Cecelia Desire, b. March 24, 1841.

277 Roanna Maria, b. January 30, 1843.

278 Alonzo Wellington, b. April 24, 1845.

279 Aurilla Emmeline, b. January 5, 1848, at Danville, Ky.

280 Sarah Josephine, b. November 21, 1852, at Fairfield, Ia., d. November 18, 1863, at Plattsmouth, Neb.

281 Mary Ellen, b. June 15, 1856, at Fairfield, Ia.

John Rathburn (Gen. IV, No. 79), b. October 30, 1823, at Jackson, O., d. April 21, 1902, at Jackson, O.; m. March 25, 1850, at Jackson, O., to Minerva Tomlinson, b. February 7, 1832.

Mr. Rathburn was known and respected as one of a group of pioneers of Jockson, O. He was a member of the Methodist Protestant church established in Jackson by his grandfather, Hon. John James.

The married life of Mr. and Mrs. Rathburn extending over a period of fifty-two years is said by

those who knew them intimately to have been an ideal one.

Mr. Rathburn will be remembered as a loyal friend, a true husband and an upright citizen.

Generation V.

Children of John and Minerva (Tomlinson) Rathburn.

282 Cornelia Virginia, b. January 23. 1852.
283 Ripley, b. June 11. 1858, unm.

Joseph Rathburn (Gen IV, No. 80), d. unmarried.

Romaine Rathburn (Gen. IV, No. 81), b. May 9, 1827, at Jackson, O. d April, 1884, at Dayton, O. (Buried at Spring Grove cemetery, Cincinnati, O.,) m. May 28, 1851, at Jackson, O, to Rev. Truman S. Cowden, D. D., Cincinnati conference.

Mrs. Cowden was a deeply religious woman and did a most effective work as the wife of a pastor. She was a great worker in the cause of temperance; converted at the age of fourteen, she united with the M. E. church.

While yet very young she became seriously ill, and after the physician had given up all hope of recovery, she, aware of her critical condition, carried her case to God in prayer; she was greatly blessed and began to praise God, whereat a reaction set in, which resulted in her complete recovery.

Generation V.

Children of T. S and Romaine (Rathburn) Cowden.

284 Emma, d. young.
285 Edgar H., b 1855, d. 1876.
286 Jennie, d. young.
287 Mary Bennett, lives at Columbus, O., unm.

288 Clifford Reedy, stenographer, lives at Columbus, O., unm
289 Anna Hayes, teacher, at Columbus, O., unm.

Charles B. Rathburn (Gen. IV, No. 82), b. 1829, at Jackson, O., d. February 7, 1875; m. (1) to Delia Lonta; m. (2) February 26, 1874, to Lissette Brockamp, b. October 31, 1843, in Germany.

Generation V.

Children of Charles and Delia (Lonta) Rathburn.

290 Joseph, b. 1856, d. unm.
291 Ida, b. 1858.

Eliza Rathburn (Gen. IV, No. 83), b. at Jackson, O.; m. (1) George Lucas; m. (2) Robert Simpson.

Generation V.

Children of George and Eliza (Rathburn) Lucas.

292 George.
293 Mary, d. in infancy.

Generation V.

Children of Robert and Eliza (Lucas) Simpson.

294 Fanny.
295 Hershel.
296 Michael.
297 Maud.
298 Lucy.

Descendants of:

Dr. Elihu and **Roanna (Rathburn) Johnson** (Gen. III, No. 22.)

George W. Johnson (Gen. IV, No. 84), b. August 7, 1835, at Jackson, O., d. about 1875, at Jackson, O.;

m. June 8, 1857, at Gallipolis, O., to Mary Ann Ridgeway, d March 11, 1898, at Chillicothe.

Services: Enlisted in U. S army June 2 1862 Was second lieutenant Company E, 87th O. V. 1. Captured by rebels at Harper's Ferry, Va., September 15, 1862. After October 3, 1862, returned home and was probate judge of Jackson county, 1864-67.

Generation V.

Children of George W. and Mary (Ridgeway) Johnson.

299 Hershel V., b. March 13, 1858.
300 Ida B., b November 12, 1859.
301 David Todd, b. September 5, 1861.
302 Joseph, d. young.

Pauline Johnson (Gen IV, No. 86), b. March 17, 1839, at Jackson, O , d November 11, 1887, at Jackson, O.; m. June 8, 1865, at Jackson, O., to James Chestnut, b. November 22, 1834.

Mrs. Chestnut was a member of the M. E. church and a woman of strong character and great ability. She presented on behalf of the women of Jackson, a silk flag to the first company of soldiers who went from Jackson to the civil war.

Generation V.

Children of James and Pauline (Johnson) Chestnut.

303 Jeanette, b. March 29, 1866
304 Katherine Estella, b July 5, 1872.
305 Charles Sumner. b. January 29, 1874.
306 Earl Acton, b January 4, 1876.

Lucretia Johnson (Gen. IV, No 87), b. October 15, 1842, at Jackson, O.; m. June 18, 1863, at Chillicothe, O., to William Simpson.

Generation V.

Children of William and Lucretia (Johnson) Simpson.

307 Charles, b. April 12. 1864, d. October 31, 1869

308 William, b. August 9, 1865, d. September 30, 1884.

309 Bailess, b. March 10, 1867, d. October 17, 1892.

Julia James Johnson (Gen. IV, No. 89), b. January 21, 1848, at Jackson. O.. lives at Jackson, O.

Descendants of:

John Denison (Gen. III, No. 23), and **Sarah (Mitchell) James.**

Authority. Family records contributed by Adaline (Miller) Ervin, No. 337.

John Ripley James (Gen. IV, No. 91), b. August 9, 1835, at Jackson, O. Was a leading hospital physician in the 2nd Virginia cavalry, 1861; d. unm. September 9, 1862, at Guyandotte, W. Va.

David M. James (Gen. IV, No. 92), b. May 25, 1837, at Jackson, O., d. unm. February 3, 1898, at Jackson, O. Admitted to the bar and served through the civil war.

Thomas Denison James (Gen. IV, No. 93), b. March 3, 1839, at Jackson, O.; m. April 5, 1871, at Brazil, Ind., to Margaret Brown. Served in civil war as trainmaster. No children.

Residence, Macon, Mo.

Nancy Cook James (Gen. IV, No. 94), b. October 3, 1840, at Jackson, O.; m. August 27, 1865, to Rev. William A. Sampson, b. February 5, 1829, d. November 5, 1892.

Generation V.

Children of Rev. Wm. A. and Nancy (James) Sampson.

310 Ida Bell, b. February 17, 1867.

311 Stella Myrtle, b. November 5, 1868.

312 Maud, b. April 22, 1872.

Charles Curtland James (Gen IV, No. 95), b. December 29, 1842, at Jackson, O., d October 21, 1901, at Jackson, O.; m. April 6, 1869, at Portsmouth, O., to Hannah E. Currie.

Residence, Jackson, O.

Generation V.

Children of Charles C. and Hannah (Currie) James.

313 Ripley Currie, b September 13, 1870.

Charles C James, who has rendered the republican party long and valuable service, is one of the best known supporters of that organization in Ohio. He enlisted his services in the war of the rebellion in 1861 as a private and was promoted to the rank of sergeant for meritorious conduct. continuing on duty until incapacitated by a wound received at the battle of Winchester and was discharged in April. 1865. He enlisted when eighteen years old in Company K, 36th Ohio volunteer in fantry, under General Cook, and participated in the battles of Lanesburg, Lookout Mountain, Antietam, Kennesaw Mountain, Winchester, Chickamauga, Mission Ridge and many others

At the conclusion of hostilities Mr. James located in Jackson, O., where he was made township clerk: was elected clerk of the county courts in 1866, filling that office two terms and for some time served as deputy clerk, altogether comprising a period of ten years in that department. He was elected mayor of Jackson three times. resigning before the expiration of his third term and took up the study of law, being admitted to the bar of Ohio in 1876, only. however, following the profession a short time In 1892 Governor McKinley appointed him warden of the Ohio penitentiary, occupying that position two years.

For many years Mr. James has been a member of the county executive committee, of which he has frequently been chosen chairman, and held that position in 1892, when he made a strong fight for Governor McKinley in Jackson county. He served one year on the state central committee and attended the state and district conventions, of which he was usually chairman.

Mr. James was born in Jackson county, Ohio, on the 29th day of December, 1842, a son of John D James. The latter was born in 1806; he affiliated with the democratic party, and his death took place in 1887, at the advanced age of eighty-one years. His grandfather was Major John James, who came to Ohio in 1807, and represented Jackson county in the state legislature. Our subject was a member of the Ohpir Iron Company, which built a charcoal furnace near Jackson, and he continued in that business until 1875, when he took charge of the Jackson Mill and Lumber Company, of which he was made president and general manager and retained that position until 1892, when his appointment as warden of the state penitentiary necessitated his resignation. After the expiration of his term of office, Mr. James returned to Jackson and once more became associated with the mill and lumber business, continuing in the same until his death

He was a man of ability and energy, progressive and reliable, and possessed the warm regard of his many friends and the entire confidence of all his business associates.   ¹

Zachariah Ragon James (Gen. IV, No. 96), b. October 16, 1844, at Jackson, O.; m. July 20, 1870, at Jackson, O., to Sarah A. Bennett, b. April 20, 1850, at Jackson, O , d. February 15, 1893, at Chicago, Ill. Zachariah R. James has been for thirty-five years superintendent of the electrical works at Chicago.

Generation V.

Children of Zachariah and Sarah (Bennett) James.

314 Oota Bell, b February 22, 1871, at Chicago, Ill

315 Silas Edward, b June 6, 1873, d October 6, 1874.

316 Florence Edna, b November 2 1877, d. at Chicago, Ill., January 15, 1910.

317 Grace Ella, b. October 31, 1878, at Chicago, Ill.

318 Sarah, b. March 6, 1880, d. September 1, 1881, at Chicago Ill.

319 Mary Beatrice, b July 6, 1887, at Chicago, Ill.

320 Elmer Clinton, b. August 13, 1890, at Chicago, Ill.

Mary Eleanor James (Gen. IV. No. 97), b. October 19, 1846, at Jackson, O , d. December 30, 1897, at Jackson, O.; m. September 23, 1873, at Jackson, O , to Samuel G. Martin.

Generation V.

Children of Samuel G. and Mary (James) Martin.

321 Lena F., b July 6, 1874, at Jackson, O.

Edward Mitchell James (Gen. IV. No. 98), b. June 4, 1848, at Jackson, O., d. August 17, 1869, at Jackson, O

Edward M. James died just after completing a course in electrical engineering.

Eliza Elizabeth James (Gen. IV, No. 99), b. March 19, 1850, at Jackson, O.; m. September 22, 1887, at Jackson, O., to Miles Jones.

Residence, Jackson, O.

Franklin James (Gen. IV, No. 100), b. January 29, 1852, at Jackson, O., unm.

79

Tryphena James (Gen. IV, No. 101), b. September 20, 1854, at Jackson, O , unm.

Ida May James (Gen. IV, No. 102), b. May 20, 1858, at Jackson, O.; m. June 12, 1883, at Jackson, O., to Edward J. Bannon.

Generation V.

Children of Edward J. and Ida (James) Bannon.

322 Sarah Marcella, b. March 16, 1885.

Descendants of ·

Alexander and **Harmeon (James) Miller** (Gen. III, No. 25.)

Authority: Family records contributed by Mary May Miller, No. 327.

Mary E. Miller (Gen. IV, No. 103), b. August 26, 1826, at Jackson, O., d. July 3, 1903, at Wellston, O.; m. Hezekiah Bundy, b. August 15, 1817, at Marietta. O., d. December 12, 1895, at Wellston, O.

Residence, Wellston, O.

Emily Miller (Gen. IV, No. 104.) b. May 6, 1828. d. August 17, 1885, m. November 13, 1850, to Anthony Burress Walker. of Brook county, Virginia.

Generation V.

Children of Anthony and Emily (Miller) Walker.

323 Frank Edwin, b. May 27, 1852.
324 Mary Belle, b. November 27, 1853.
325 Lucy Matilda, b. February 3, 1859.
326 David Anthony, b. July 8, 1861.

Captain David Allen Miller (Gen. IV, No. 107), b. April 25, 1835, at Jackson, O., d February 6, 1891, at Logan, O.; m (1) October 12, 1865, to Lucinda Rath-

burn, d. December 9. 1875, at Logan, O.; m. (2) September 2, 1881, to Sarepta Davis.

Residence, Logan, O.

Captain David A Miller enlisted in Company H, 75th Ohio infantry; promoted to sergeant, then to first lieutenant, wounded at Gettysburg, July 1, 1863, and discharged. Returning to Logan, O., he was first appointed collector. then superintendent of the Hocking canal. Member of I O O. F, and K. of P.

Generation V.

Children of David A. and Lucinda (Rathburn) Miller.

   327 Mary May, b. December 11, 1867.

   328 Lucinda Jane, b October 29, 1869.

   329 Georgia, b October 13, 1872.

Generation V.

Children of David A. and Sarepta (Davis) Miller.

   330 Besse Elizabeth, b. June 3, 1882.

Maria Miller (Gen. IV, No 108), b. July 10. 1837, at Jackson, O., d. February 14, 1894, at Chillicothe, O.; m. February 8, 1854, to Samuel H. Books.

Residence, Chillicothe, O.

Generation V.

Children of Samuel H. and Maria (Miller) Books.

   331 Linnie May, b. September 11, 1855.

   332 Mary Flora, b. September 3, 1857, died.

   333 Oscar E., b. September 14, 1859

   334 David T., b. February 17, 1862.

   335 Samuel H., b. April 7, 1864.

   336 Frank E., b. March 23, 1866.

Alonzo Miller (Gen. IV, No. 109), b. January 14, 1844, at Jackson, O , m April 29, 1867, at Jackson, O.,

to Elizabeth Rooke, b December 25, 1841, near Jackson, O.

Residence, Jackson, O.

Services: Enlisted July 27, 1863, to serve three years or during the civil war. Was a private in Company K, commanded by Captain W. S. Bradford in 2nd regiment of Ohio heavy artillery volunteers commanded by Colonel Gibson Discharged August 23, 1865, at Nashville, Tenn.

Generation V.

Children of Alonzo and Elizabeth (Rooke) Miller.

337 Mary Adaline, b. March 14, 1868.

338 Emily Annette, b September 14, 1869.

339 Bertha May, b. September 10, 1871.

340 David Allen, b. March 14, 1874.

341 Caroline Bundy, b. March 10, 1876.

342 Jesse Jerome, b. July 1, 1878, d. October 11, 1882.

343 Elizabeth Rooke, b. October 13, 1881.

Addie Miller (Gen. IV, No. 110), b. August 1, 1850, m. May 12, 1868, at McArthur, O., to George Allen Gold.

Residence, Sedalia, Mo.

Generation V.

Children of George A. and Addie (Miller) Gold.

344 May Maria, b. March 31, 1869.

345 Laura Jane, b. January 12, 1871, d. September 27, 1872.

346 William Conrad, b. April 28, 1873.

347 Harriet Pearl, b. December 12, 1875.

348 George Leonard, b. June 24, 1879.

349 Earl Samuel, b. January 12, 1885.

Descendants of:

Andrew and **Eliza** (James) **Long** (Gen. III, No. 26.)

Authority: Family records contributed by Adaline M. Ervin, No. 337

Amanda Long (Gen IV, No. 111), b. August 28, 1832, at Jackson, O., m. November 13, 1850, at Jackson, O., to Rev. Lewis Allen Atkinson.

Generation V.

Children of Rev. Lewis and Amanda (Long) Atkinson.

350 Charles Andrew, b. February 9, 1852.

351 Eliza Long, b. May 1, 1856.

352 Mary, b. August 4, 1858, d. September 7, 1859

353 Caroline Bundy, b. March 1, 1866.

Elias Long (Gen. IV, No. 112), b. November 30, 1835, at Jackson, O ; m. Emma Carrick.

Authority: Family records contributed by C. A. Long, No. 367.

Generation V.

Children of Elias and Emma (Carrick) Long.

354 Lilly Dale, b. March 17, 1862.

355 Eliza James, b. December 8, 1863.

356 Effie Alice, b. August 27, 1865.

357 Amanda L., b September 30, 1867.

358 Andrew A., b. December 12, 1869.

359 Elizabeth L., b. January 19, 1872.

360 Nellie Boles, b March 18, 1874.

361 Mary Frances, b. July 15, 1876

362 Edna, b. August 23, 1878, d. 1880.

363 Infant son, b. August 19, 1880, d. August 24, 1880.

John James Long (Gen. IV, No. 113.), b. February 13, 1842, at Jackson, O.; m. June 12, 1863, to Sarah E. McNeil, d. May 18, 1887.

Authority. Family records contributed by C. A. Long, No. 367.

Generation V.

Children of John J. and Sarah (McNeil) Long.

364 John F., b. December 7, 1864, d. August 14, 1867.

365 William, b. November 28, 1866, d. November 28, 1866.

366 Cornelia V, b. March 27, 1868.

367 Charles A. b. August 8, 1870.

368 Luiza E, b. June 18, 1874.

Jacob A. Long (Gen. IV, No. 114), b. February 24, 1847, at Jackson, O ; m. October 10, 1870, at Chillicothe, O., to Ella Dascomb, b. July 22, 1849, d. May 6 1908, at Jackson, O.

Residence, Jackson, O.

In 1868 Jacob A. Long was appointed deputy auditor, stockholder and director of Iron National Bank.

Authority: Family records contributed by Adaline M. Ervin, No. 337.

Generation V.

Children of Jacob A. and Ella (Dascomb) Long.

369 Frank J., b. September 1, 1871.

370 Eliza Flora, b. February 3, 1874.

371 Charles C., b. September 18, 1879, d. August 22, 1905.

372 Daisy, b. March 9, 1882.

373 James Denison, b. April 5, 1886.

374 Howard J., b. October 11, 1889.

Descendants of ·

Paul (Gen. III, No. 28), and **Julia (Kincheloe) Cooke.**

Authority, family records contributed by Mrs. Clara B. McCluer, No. 131.

Harriet Cooke (Gen. IV, No. 115), b. January 6, 1833, probably at Worthington Creek, W. Va., d. February 16 1864; m. October 8, 1855, to George A. Welles, civil engineer.

Residence, Parkersburg, W. Va.

Generation V.

Children of George A. and Harriet (Cooke) Welles.

375 Julia Mary, b. about 1856.
376 Harriet Aurelia, b. 1861.
377 Clara, b. 1863.

Sarah Cooke (Gen. IV, No. 116), b. November 14, 1834, in West Virginia; m. October 21, 1858, to Rathbone Van Winkle, attorney-at-law; d. 1870.

Residence, Parkersburg, W. Va.

Generation V.

Children of Rathbone and Sarah (Cooke) Van Winkle.

378 Munson Cooke, b. February 4, 1860.
379 Henry Cooke, b. November 2, 1862.
380 Juliette, b. August 14, 1866.
381 Harriette, b. August 6, 1868.

Maria Cooke (Gen. IV, No. 117), b. November 11, 1836, in West Virginia; m. September 18, 1867, to Henry Amiss, attorney-at-law, d. October 8, 1894.

Residence, Parkersburg, W. Va.

85

Generation V.

Children of Henry and Maria (Cooke) Amiss.

382 Bettie, b. July 5, 1868, d August 3, 1869.

383 Anne Adelaide, b. December 8, 1870.

384 Sarah Van Winkle, b. July 18, 1874, d. April 24, 1894.

Henry C. Cooke (Gen. IV. No. 118), b. May 11, 1839, d. unm. June 25, 1864.

Enlisted with Company II, 36th Virginia infantry army of confederate states of America on August 2, 1862. Wounded at Battle of Piedmont.

Mary F. Cooke (Gen. IV, No. 119), b. October 31, 1841, in West Virginia, d September 7, 1881; m. October 21, 1868, to Edward Lyman Welles, d. 1868.

Hannah Cooke (Gen IV, No. 120), b. November 8, 1843, d. August 26, 1902; m. October 21, 1868, to W. W. Van Winkle.

Generation V.

Children of W. W. and Hannah (Cooke) Van Winkle

385 Mary, b. January 18, 1871.

Descendants of:

Bennett (Gen. III, No. 30), and **Julia (Devol) Cooke.**

Authority: Family records contributed by Mrs. Clara B McCluer, No. 131.

Frances V. Cooke (Gen. IV, No. 122), b. September 4; 1843, m. John R. Ebert.

Generation V.

Children of John R. and Frances (Cooke) Ebert.

386 Charles.

Letha Devol Cooke (Gen. IV, No. 124), b. March 10, 1848, d. 1906; m. George II. Gordon.

Generation V.

Children of George II. and Letha (Cooke) Gordon.

387 Harry.

Descendants of:

Hon. John James (Gen. III, No. 31), and **Sophia (Kincheloe) Cooke.**

Authority: Family records contributed by Clara B. McCluer, No. 131.

Fanny M. Cooke (Gen. IV, No. 128), b. July 21, 1846, probably at Parkersburg, W. Va.; m. December 6, 1870, to Frank L. Hammond.

Residence, Ellicott City, Md.

Generation V.

Children of Frank L. and Fanny (Cooke) Hammond.

388 Mary Carr, b. July 31, 1872.

389 Sophia, b. November 10, 1875.

390 Lillian, b. January 5, 1878.

391 James, b. August 3, 1880.

392 Frank Lloyd, b. April 1884.

393 William, b. March, 1887.

394 Eleanor, b. January 16, 1892.

Clara Bettie Cook (Gen. IV, No. 131), b. January 29, 1854, at Parkersburg, W. Va.; m. September 12, 1876, to Judge John Grigsby McCluer.

Residence, Parkersburg, W. Va.

WAR RECORD OF JOHN GRIGSBY M'CLUER.

J G McCluer is a native of Rockbridge county, Virginia. Was a student in 1861, at Washington college, now Washington and Lee university. He joined the Rockbridge artillery,

a company raised at Lexington, Virginia This company was made up of a number of members of the Episcopal church, at Lexington, Virginia, of which Rev Dr. Pendleton was pastor He afterwards became brigadier general and was the chief of artillery under Gen Robert E Lee.

The company was ordered to Harpers Ferry, Virginia, and reached there about April 15th, and was connected with the Stonewall brigade, which was formed about the 1st or 2nd of July, and was known then as the first brigade commanded by Gen Thomas J. Jackson (Stonewall Jackson), who had been promoted from major to brigadier general

The first engagement was with General Patterson's advance guard, about five miles below Martinsburg in the Shenandoah valley, and which engagement was on the 3rd of June.

The Confederates fell back to Winchester, and on the 16th started to join General Beauregard at Manasas or Bull Run, which point was reached by our command on the night of the 20th of July, and on the 21st the Rockbridge battery supported by Jackson's brigade was placed on Henry's hill; and was opposed by the batteries of Rickets and Griffin. It was within but a few yards of the location of this battery that General Bee fell mortally wounded, and gave to the first brigade the name of "Stonewall," by which name it was known during the entire war.

Was with Gen. Stonewall Jackson and his command in the Romney campaign Was at the battle of McDowell In the reorganization of the army, after the twelve months enlistment had expired, he changed his service from the artillery to cavalry, and joined Company B, of the twelfth Virginia cavalry. Was with Jackson in his Valley campaign against Banks Was in the battle near Winchester. Was in the battle at Barton's Mills

Was in the fight at Chancellorsville, the Wilderness and Fredericksburg, and the cavalry fight at Brandy Station, in which comparatively all of the cavalry of both armies were engaged Was in the second battle of Manassas. Was also in the fight at Jack's Shop; also, at Cedar Mountain. Afterwards, detailed on special duty at the instance of General Butler, of South Carolina, and sent with the scouts of General Hampton in rear of the Federal forces about Petersburg, operated in the rear of these lines for about four months between James river and the Nansmond river, when an

order came for relief from that service, and was ordered to report to General Rosser, in the valley of Virginia.

In coming through the enemy's lines, near what is known as the Proctor House, on Jerusalem Plank road, below Petersburg, he was captured at 2 o'clock in the morning of September 13, 1864. The Confederate pickets at that point having been captured by the Union forces, and a company of Pennsylvania cavalry placed there in its stead. Was sent to City Point, where he remained for about one month, in what was known as the Bull Pen, and from there was sent as a prisoner to Point Lookout, where he remained until he was exchanged on account of sickness and sent up James river and through the lines to Richmond in February 1864. Was paroled and returned to his home in Rockbridge county, and when his parole expired left on the same evening to join his command which was then, as he was informed, in the neighborhood of Richmond. But, upon reaching Lynchburg, Virginia, he learned of General Lee's surrender at Appomatox. He then returned to his home at Lexington, Virginia.

Generation V.

Children of John and Clara (Cook) McCluer.

395 James Steele, b. November 15, 1877.
396 John Cameron, b. September 15, 1879.
397 Henry Randolph, b. March 15, 1882.
398 John Grigsby, b. August 11, 1884.
399 Earl Hamilton, b. January 11, 1887.
400 Lawrence Moss, b. July 6, 1889.
401 Mary Cooke, b. December 14, 1891.
402 Charles Forrer Anderson, b. February 26, 1895.

Julia Cooke (Gen. IV, No. 133), b. April 27, 1863, at Parkersburg, W. Va.; m. January 6, 1898, to Smith D. Turner.

Generation V.

Children of Smith D. and Julia (Cooke) Turner.

403 Smith D., b. August 10, 1904.

Descendants of:

Jacob and Melissa (Paine) Hawk (Gen. III, No. 34.

Authority: Family records contributed by Amanda Hawk, No. 136.

Frances Asberry Hawk (Gen. IV, No 134), b. December 25, 1831, at Wilkesville, O., d. July 5, 1889, at Wilkesville, O., unm.

Melissa Abigail Hawk (Gen IV, No. 135), b. March 5, 1834, at Wilkesville, O., d. August 21, 1893, at Wilkesville, O., unm.

Amanda Eleanor Hawk (Gen. IV, No. 136), b. August 2, 1836, at Wilkesville, O.; m. September 28, 1865, to R. W. Strong.

James Monroe Hawk (Gen IV, No. 137), b. July 4, 1840, at Wilkesville, O , d. at Shelton, Neb.; m. September 21, 1865, at Hamden, O., to Rebecca Emma Beard, d. 1873; m. (2) May 8, 1884, at Atlantic, Ia., to Mary A. Marriott.

Residence, Wilkesville, O.; Shelton, Neb.

Generation V.

Children of James M. and Emma (Beard) Hawk.

404 Eugene Owen, b. August 5, 1866, d. March 18, 1880.

Generation V.

Children of James M. and Mary (Marriott) Hawk.

405 Lillie Melissa, b. April 11, 1885.
406 Francis Wilmot, b. June 18, 1888.
407 George Clifford, b. November 10, 1890.
408 Stella, b. May 4, 1897.

Caroline Paine Hawk (Gen. IV, No. 138), b. June 27, 1842, at Wilkesville, O., d. about 1886; m April 4, 1865, at Wilkesville, O., to J. C. Coffman, officer in U. S. army.

Generation V.

Children of J. C. and Caroline (Hawk) Coffman.

409 Claude, d. at age of two years.

Mary E. Hawk (Gen. IV, No. 139), b October 3, 1844, at Wilkesville, O.; m. February 12, 1866, at Wilkesville, O., to David F. Hover.

Residence, Decatur, Ill.

Generation V.

Children of David F. and Mary (Hawk) Hover.

410 Clarence A., b. June 3, 1867; m. and lives at Kansas City, Mo.

411 Blanche C., b. April 4. 1869. d. January 1, 1903, at Decatur, Ill

Elizabeth Ophelia Hawk (Gen. IV, No. 140), b. February 21, 1847, at Wilkesville, O., d. November 7, 1881; m. December 25, 1873, at Wilkesville, O., to J. R. Bagby.

David Wilmot Hawk (Gen. IV, No. 141), b. June 2, 1850, at Wilkesville, O , d. unm. at Wilkesville, O., June 22, 1901.

Descendants of:

Lemuel Shepherd (Gen. III, No. 35), and Elizabeth (Roby) Paine.

Authority: Family records contributed by Clara (Paine) Ohler, No. 148.

James Basil Paine (Gen. IV, No. 143), b. October 1, 1844, at Hamden, O., d. September 20, 1883, at Ham-

den, O., m. (1) November 4, 1874, at Greenfield, O., to Fannie W. Allen, b. about 1852, at Greenfield, O., d. November 28, 1875, at Hayesville, O.; m. (2) February 25, 1879, at Jackson, O., to Cornelia Dickason, b. December 5, 1856, in Jackson county, Ohio; lives at Jackson, O.

Residence, Hamden, O.; Jackson, O.

Graduate of Ohio Wesleyan University, 1871; member of Phi Kappa Psi fraternity; superintendent of schools at Greenfield, O.; representative of Jackson county in Ohio legislature in 1878 and 1880; attorney-at-law.

Generation V.

Children of James B. and Fannie (Allen) Paine.

412 William, b. 1875, d. at six months.

Generation V.

Children of James B. and Cornelia (Dickason) Paine.

413 Fannie Elizabeth, b. July 9, 1881.
414 James Basil, b August 8, 1883.

David Sanford Paine (Gen. IV, No. 144), b. **August** 23, 1846, at Hamden, O., d. unm. January 4, 1876.

Bennett Roby Paine (Gen. IV, No. 145), b. August 27, 1848, at Hamden O.; m. October 15, 1878, at Hamden, O., to Alice L. Wilcox, b. December 5, 1852, at Allensville, O.

Residence, Hamden, O.

Generation V.

Children of Bennett R. and Alice (Wilcox) Paine.

415 Howard Shepard, b. May 12, 1880.
416 Joseph Arthur, b. May 16, 1886, d. January 29, 1889.

417 Lawrence Wilcox, b. April 17, 1890.

Delia Elizabeth Paine (Gen. IV, No. 146), b. March 4, 1851, at Hamden, O.

Residence, Lima, O , Shepard, O.

Graduate of Ohio Wesleyan Seminary; member of D. A. R. 1906.

William Denison Paine (Gen. IV, No. 147), b. October 7, 1860, at Hamden, O , d. unm. September 21 1883, at Hamden, O.

Clara May Paine (Gen. IV, No. 148), b. July 24, 1862, at Hamden, O.; m. October 15, 1884, at Hamden, O., to James Oswell Ohler, b. September 27, 1859, in Hardin county, Ohio.

Residence, Lima, O.

Educated at Wesleyan College, Cincinnati, O., and O. W. U. at Delaware, O., member of D. A. R., 1904 and founder of Lima Chapter, 1907; member of Society of Colonial Dames, 1907; member of Society of Founders and Patriots, 1911. Author of this genealogy.

Generation. V.

Children of James O. and Clara (Paine) Ohler.

418 Katherine, b. November 9, 1887.
419 Elizabeth Roby, b. March 24, 1889.
420 Willard Paine, b. May 30 1891.
Descendants of:

John N. and **Sarah (Paine) Hurst** (Gen. III, No. 37.)

Authority: Family records contributed by J. M. Hurst, No. 153.

David L. Hurst (Gen IV, No 149), b. July 8, 1834. in Ross county, O.; m. March 10, 1857, at Harrisburg,

O., to Emeline Dalby, b. October 27, 1840, at Harrisburg, O.

Residence, Columbus, O.

Generation V.

Children of David L. and Emeline (Dalby) Hurst.

421 Clyde W., b. April 13, 1858
422 Caroline E., b. March 27, 1861.
423 Joseph N., b. July 5, 1862.
424 S. Louise, b. August 4, 1864.

Wilson R. Hurst (Gen. IV, No. 151), b. December 23, 1837, in Ross county, O.; m. May 27, 1867, at Piketon, O., to Ella Patterson, b June 30, 1850.

Residence, Piketon, O

Generation V.

Children of Wilson R. and Ella (Patterson) Hurst.

425 Mellie, b. November 1, 1870.
426 C. Scott b. April 5, 1873.
427 Lulu Catherine, b. September 21, 1876
428 Carrie Grace, b. January 18, 1880.

Caroline L. Hurst (Gen. IV, No. 152), b. March 24, 1839. in Ross county, Ohio, d. March 15, 1892, in Ross county, Ohio.; m. August 26. 1885, in Ross county, Ohio, to George Morrow, b July 17, 1819, at Jefferson, O., d. March 15 1908, in Ross county, Ohio.

Joseph M. Hurst (Gen. IV, No 153), b. February 7, 1841, in Ross county, Ohio, m. November 17, 1869, at Kingston, O., to Catherine S. Little, b July 24, 1846, at Chillicothe, O.

Residence, Williamsport, O.

Generation V.

Children of Joseph M. and Catherine (Little) Hurst.
429 Lemuel J., b. April 14, 1871.
430 Carl L., b. February 10. 1877.
431 Elwin L., b. February 10, 1877.

Amanda Hurst (Gen. IV, No. 154), b. November 19, 1843, in Ross county, Ohio, unm.
Residence, Ross county, Ohio.

Douglas T. Hurst (Gen. IV , No. 155), b. October 2, 1846, in Ross county, Ohio; m. September 11, 1878, to Laura Morrow. b May 7, 1860, in Ross county, Ohio, d. November 9, 1906.

Generation V.

Children of Douglas T. and Laura (Morrow) Hurst.
432 Ethel M., b. June 11, 1882.
433 Gilbert S , b. May 31, 1885.
434 R. Harold, b. March 4, 1893.
435 George N., b. October 21, 1891, d. January 28, 1892.

Charles B. Hurst (Gen. IV, No. 156), b. May 11, 1852, in Ross county, Ohio; m. September 20, 1876, at Chillicothe, O., to Ella Warner, b. July 25, 1852.
Residence, Chillicothe, O.

Generation V.

Children of Charles B. and Ella (Warner) Hurst.
436 Myrtle, b. March 21, 1881.
437 Roy W., b. March 11, 1886.
Descendants of:

Jonathan Douglas (Gen. III, No. 38), and **Julia (Hurst) Paine.**

Authority: Family records contributed by Elizabeth (Paine) Cherrington, No. 157. .

Elizabeth Ophelia Paine (Gen. IV, No. 157), b. August 3, 1841, in Jackson county, Ohio, m. December 25, 1867, at Delaware, O., to Rev. George W. Cherrington. b. May 30, 1842, at Evergreen, O., d. November 7, 1900, at Evergreen, O.

Residence, various towns in Ohio.

Generation V.

Children of George and Elizabeth (Paine) Cherrington.

438 William Douglas, b. and d. September 24, 1870, at Ewington, O.

439 Arthur Paine, b. October 10, 1871.

440 Wanita Grace, b. April 12, 1874.

441 Stella Janet, b. January 16, 1876, at Letart, O., d September 30, 1884, at Piketon, O.

442 Ernest Hurst, b. November 24, 1877.

443 Edith Chone, b. January 10, 1880.

444 Laura, b. and d. January 1, 1883, at Wheelers-burgh, O.

Descendants of:

Hezekiah S. and **Caroline (Paine) Bundy** (Gen. III, No. 39.

Authority: Family records contributed by Julia (Bundy) Foraker, No. 159.

Julia Ann Paine Bundy (Gen. IV, No. 159), b. June 17, 1847, in Jackson county, Ohio; m. October 4. 1870, in Jackson county, Ohio. to Captain Joseph Benson Foraker, b. July 5, 1846, at Hillsboro, O.

Residence, Washington, D. C. and Cincinnnati, O.

Julia (Bundy) Foraker graduated from the Ohio Wesleyan Female Seminary, in 1868. Member of D. A. R., 1904; state vice regent in 1905 and 1906; member of Society of Colonial Dames of America in 1905; member of Society of Founders and Patriots, 1911.

Joseph Benson Foraker enlisted in Company A,

89th regiment O. V. I.; at close of the civil war he was first lieutenant and brevet captain; graduated from Cornell University in 1869; admitted to the bar 1869, elected judge of superior court of Cincinnati. April, 1879; elected governor of Ohio in 1885; re-elected in 1887; chairman of the republican state conventions of Ohio for 1886, 1890, 1896, 1900 and 1901; delegate at large from Ohio to the national republican convention of 1884, 1888, 1892, 1896, 1900 and 1904; was chairman of the Ohio delegation in the convention of 1884 and 1888 and presented to both of these conventions the name of Hon. John Sherman for nomination to the presidency.

In the conventions of 1892 and 1896, served as chairman of the committee on resolutions and reported the platform to the conventions and presented the name of William McKinley to the conventions of 1896 and 1900 for nomination to the presidency; was elected United States senator January 15, 1896, and re-elected January 15, 1902, to succeed himself. At the expiration of his term of office, March 3, 1909, he resumed the practice of law at Cincinnati, O.

Generation V.

Children of Joseph B. and Julia (Bundy) Foraker.

445 Joseph Benson, Jr., b. July 23, 1872.
446 Florence M., b. September 14, 1874.
447 Clara Louise, b October 16, 1876.
448 Julia Bundy, b. January 31, 1880.
449 Arthur St. Clair, b. April 26, 1892.

Eliza Melinda Bundy (Gen. IV, No. 160), b. June 17, 1850, in Jackson county, Ohio; m June, 1871, at Erie, Pa., to Harvey Wells, b. at Wilkesville, O., d. at Wellston, O.

Residence, Washington, D. C.

Generation V.

Children of Harvey and Eliza (Bundy) Wells.
450 Harry, b. May 30, 1877.
Descendants of:

Frederic and Maria (Bailey) Shipman (Gen. III, No. 40.)

Authority: Family records contributed by Ellen F. Bailey, No. 190.

Mary Sibyl Shipman (Gen. IV, No. 161), b. December 28, 1830, at Marietta, O.; m. (1) 1851, to John Ross Everett, d 1852; m. (2) August 12, 1856, to Byron Sloper, d. October 14, 1885, at Elmdale, Kan.

Residence, Marietta, O.; Elmdale, Kan.

Generation V.

Children of John R. and Mary (Shipman) Everett.
451 Harriet Anna Maria, b. September, 1852.

Generation V.

Children of Byron and Mary (Everett) Sloper.
452 Carrie, b. October 15, 1857, d. March 10, 1864, at Leavenworth, Kan.

Joshua Seth Shipman (Gen. IV, No. 162), b March 6, 1832, at Marietta, O., d. March 1889, at Elmdale, Kan.; m. (1) September 9, 1856, at Athens. O., to Sarah Carpenter, daughter of Frederic and Mary Carpenter, d. July 23, 1858; m. (2) August 8, 1864, in Chase county, Kansas, to Jennie Gifford, d. 1874, at Elmdale, Kan.; m. (3) September 24, 1876, at Cedar Point, Kan., to Addie Seamans, daughter of Alvin and Almira Seamans, b. at Wheaton, Ill.

Generation V.

Children of Joshua S. and Sarah (Carpenter) Shipman.
453 Charles Frederic, b. July, 1857.

98

Generation V.

Children of Joshua S. and Jennie (Gifford) Shipman.

4£4 Julia Sloper.

455 Arthur Bartlett.

456 Annie Maud.

457 Minnie, b. April 5, 1872, d. August 1, 1873.

Generation V.

Children of Joshua S. and Addie(Seamans) Shipman.

458 Harry Leroy.

Julia Maria Shipman (Gen. IV, No. 163), b. February, 23, 1835, at Marietta, O., d. March 2, 1862, at St. Joseph, Mo.; m. (1) John Lyons; m. (2) Captain A. J. Merritt.

Descendants of:

Seth (Gen III, No. 42), and **Sarah (McClure) Bailey.**

Authority: Family records contributed by Ellen Frances Bailey, No. 190.

Mary Bailey (Gen. IV, No. 165), m. Martin Van Buren Athey.

Generation V.

Children of Martin and Mary (Bailey) Athey.

459 John O.

460 Bertha Adelaide.

461 William.

Descendants of:

Seth and **Mary (Scott) Bailey.**

Authority: Family records contributed by Ellen F. Bailey, No. 190.

Nancy Ann Bailey (Gen. IV, No. 166), m. December 25, 1884, to Henry Mathias.

Lydia Jane Bailey (Gen. IV, No. 168), m. June 16, 1871, to David B. Sinclair.

99

Generation V.

Children of David and Lydia (Bailey) Sinclair.
462 Rodney Boise.
463 John North, d. May 15, 1896.
464 Ella Richmond.
465 Hunter B.
466 Mary Gertrude.

Seth Austin Bailey (Gen. IV, No. 170), m. March 24, 1892, to Elizabeth Claggett.

Julia Augusta Bailey (Gen. IV, No. 171), m. (1) March 24, 1874, to Beverly Douglas, d. September 23, 1874, m. (2) June 2, 1885, to Newton Perry, d. June, 1887.

Generation V.

Children of John B. and Julia (Bailey) Douglas.
467 John Beverly, Jr., m. and lives in Kansas.

Alice Rosetta Bailey (Gen. IV, No. 172), d. 1907. Descendants of:

John James (Gen. III, No. 44) and Mary (Chapman) Bailey.

Authority: Family records contributed by Ellen Frances Bailey, No. 190.

Sarah Bailey (Gen. IV, No. 174), b. July 8, 1838; m. May 13, 1857, to Robert Marshall Hunter, b. January 21, 1830, at Cumberland, O.

Residence, Neoga, Ill.

Generation V.

Children of Robert and Sarah (Bailey) Hunter.
468 Mary Annette, b. August 29, 1858, d. August 28, 1865.
469 Martha Aurelia, b. September 15, 1860.
470 Carrie.
471 Charles Robert, b. March 5, 1884, d. October 22, 1865.

472 Lucy Lorena.

473 Nellie.

474 Howard Bailey.

475 Sarah Ethel.

476 Anna Harriet.

John Worthington Bailey (Gen. IV, No. 175), m. November, 1879, at Constitution, O., to Louise Carpenter.

Residence, Rock Hill, Mo.

Generation V.

Children of John W. and Louise (Carpenter) Bailey.

477 John.

478 Mary Annette.

479 Bertha.

480 Mabel. ..

Descendants of:

Dr. G. A. and Susan (Bailey) Ward (Gen. III. No. 45.)

Authority: Family records contributed by Ellen Frances Bailey, No. 190.

Frances Elizabeth Ward (Gen. IV, No. 178), m. Robert Lamb. (She died early, leaving a son.)

George Rollin Ward (Gen. IV, No. 179), m. ——— Lamb (sister to Robert Lamb.)

Mary Celeste Ward (Gen. IV, No. 181), m. ——— Allen.

Walter Payson Ward (Gen. IV, No. 182), m. ——— (Name of wife unknown.)

Henry Ward (Gen. IV, No. 183), m. Jennie Anderson, daughter of Marcus Anderson.

Descendants of:

Bennett Cook (Gen. III, No. 46), and Fannie (Dickey) Bailey.

Authority: Family records contributed by Ellen Frances Bailey, No. 190.

Bennett Augustus Bailey (Gen. IV, No. 188), m. February 5, 1896, at Topeka, Kan., to Mary Margaret Horne, b. at Cincinnati, O.

Generation V.

Children of Bennett and Mary (Horne) Bailey.
481 Bennett Augustus, Jr.

Descendants of ·

William Denison (Gen. III, No. 47), and **Mary (Ward) Bailey.**

Authority: Family records contributed by Ellen F. Bailey, No. 190.

Mary Annette Bailey (Gen. IV, No. 189), b. in Washington county, Ohio, d. June 11, 1875, at Lincoln, Neb., m. June 30, 1870, to James Pennock Walton, son of Rev. James and Clara (Carter) Walton.

Generation V.

Children of James and Mary (Bailey) Walton.
482 Mary Emerson.

Descendants of:

William Denison and Elizabeth (Emerson) Bailey.

Ellen Frances Bailey (Gen. IV, No. 190), lives with her mother at Marietta, O.

Charles Emerson Bailey (Gen. IV, No. 193), m. October 9, 1900, to Elizabeth Davidson, daughter of Joshua and Helen Dudley Davidson, of Parkersburg, W. Va. Graduate of Marietta colloge. Engineer, connected with iron mines on Mesaba Range, Minn.

Generation V.

Children of Charles Emerson and Elizabeth (Davidson) Bailey.
483 Emerson Dudley.

484 Helen Elizabeth.

Descendants of:

George Washington (Gen. III, No. 48), and Sarah (Stapleton) Bailey.

Authority: Family records contributed by Ellen Frances Bailey, No. 190

Sarah Bertha Bailey (Gen. IV, No. 194), b. at Constitution, O.; m. Lewis Boardman, son of Dana Boardman.

Generation V.
Children of Lewis and Sarah (Bailey) Boardman.
485 Sarah Grace.
486 Bessie.
487 Bailey.
488 Burton.

Eliza Alberta Bailey (Gen. IV, No. 195), m. Arthur Maxwell Mattoon.

Residence, Parkville, Mo. (Professor Mattoon was a student at Cambridge, England, and has charge of observatory at Industrial school.

Generation V.
Children or Arthur and Eliza (Bailey) Mattoon.
489 Edith.
490 Arthur Maxwell, Jr.
491 Winifred.

George Howard Bailey (Gen. IV, No. 197), b. at Constitution, O., m. Lissa Bailey.

Residence, Seattle, Wash.

George H. Bailey is a graduate of the Law school at Ann Arbor, Mich., where his wife was also a student.

Generation V.
Children of George H. and Lissa (Bailey) Bailey.
492 Dorothy.

493 George Howard, Jr.

Descendants of ·

Augustus Stone (Gen. III. No. 44), and Julia (Johnson) Bailey.

Authority: Family records contributed by Ellen Frances Bailey (Gen. IV, No. 190.)

Emma Bailey (Gen. IV, No. 198), b. at Constitution, O.; m. April 7, 1886, to Clarence David Wood, b. at West Liberty, Ia., son of Stephen and Caroline (Breese) Wood.

Generation V.

Children of Clarence D. and Emma (Bailey) Wood.

494 Rhuy Bailey.

495 Howard Bailey.

496 Paul Bailey.

497 Rachel Bailey.

498 Carrie Bailey.

Clara Katharine Bailey (Gen. IV, No. 199), b. at Constitution, O.; m. June 17, 1885, to Lafe Budd Breese, b. in Ohio, son of Edwin Hatfield and Harriet (Talmage) Breese.

Generation V.

Children of Lafe B. and Clara (Bailey) Breese.

499 Julia M. b. February 15, 1887, at Elmdale, Kan., d. March 4, 1904, at San Antonio, Texas.

CHAPTER V.

Generations V and VI.

Descendants of:

James (Gen. IV, No. 56), and Laura (DeVaughn) Bailey.

Authority: Family records contributed by Laura (DeVaughn) Bailey.

Charles P. Bailey (Gen. V. No. 210), b. about 1873, in Wood county, Virginia, m. about 1896, to Lizzie Campbell.

Residence, Marietta, O.

Generation VI.

Children of Charles P. and Lizzie (Campbell) Bailey.

500 Walter, b. 1897.

Bessie Bailey (Gen. V, No. 211), b. December 4, 1875, in Wood county, Virginia; m. M. P. Hite.

Residence, Cincinnati, O.

Descendants of:

Ripley C. (Gen. IV, No. 63), and **Lucy (Fuller) Hoffman.**

Authority: Family records contributed by James Fuller Hoffman, No. 227.

James Fuller Hoffman (Gen. V, No. 227), b. August 12, 1844; m. (1) at Jackson, O., to Frank C. Watterhouse, b. July 20, 1844, daughter of Aaron and Emily Watterhouse; d. October 7, 1883, at Columbus, O.; m. (2)' July 8, 1885, at Columbus, O., to Victoria Ely, b. October 31, 1852, at Lattasville, O., daughter of Wilson and Mary Ely.

Residence, Columbus, O. and Eureka, Kan.

Generation VI.

Children of James F. and Frank (Watterhouse) Hoffman. '

501 Ripley C., b. January 4, 1873, at Columbus, O., lives near, Eureka, Kan.

502 Edith Frances, b. June 14, 1876, at Columbus, O., d. September 16, 1893, near Eureka, Kan.

Generation VI.

Children of James F. and Victoria (Ely) Hoffman.

503 Daniel, b. July 27, 1886, at Columbus, O.

504 Mary Ely, b. October 27, 1887, near Eureka, Kan.

Descendants of:

Ripley C. (Gen. IV, No. 63), and **Mary (Sullivant) Hoffman.**

Authority: Family records contributed by Arthur S. Hoffman, No. 231.

Arthur Sullivant Hoffman (Gen. V, No. 231), b. September 28, 1876, at Columbus, O.; m. October 14, 1905, at Coshocton, O., to Mary Denver James, b. February 15, 1873, at Coshocton, O.; d. August 17, 1910, at New York city.

Residence, New York.

Generation VI.

Children of Arthur S. and Mary (James) Hoffman.

505 Lyne Starling Sullivant, b. August 12, 1910, in New York.

Descendants of:

David A. (Gen. IV, No. 64), and **Emily (Smith) Hoffman.**

Authority: Family records contributed by D. A. Hoffman, No. 64.

Edgar Brown Hoffman (Gen. V, No. 232), b. August, 25, 1849. married and has a family.

John Adams Hoffman (Gen. V, No. 233), b. April 23, 1851, married and has a family.

Effie Louise Hoffman (Gen. V, No. 234), b. May 14, 1853, married to Mr. Rogers, lives at Oskaloosa, Ia.

Ripley Christian Hoffman (Gen. V. No. 235), b. November 12, 1860, married and has a family; practicing physician at Oskaloosa, Ia.

Descendants of:

John L. and Cornelia (Hoffman) Long (Gen. IV, No. 66.)

Authority: Family records contributed by Adaline M. Ervin, No. 337.

Grace Correll Long (Gen. V, No. 238), b. November 9, 1861, at Jackson O.; m. April 10, 1889, at Jackson, O., to John L. Kibbee, b. April 10, 1860, at Jackson, O.

Residence, Jackson, O.

Generation VI.

Children of John L. and Grace (Long) Kibbee.

506 John Long, b. April 10, 1890, at Jackson, O.

507 Elizabeth, b. September 7, 1900, at Jackson, O.

Harry Hoffman Long (Gen. V, No. 239), b. March 27, 1866, at Jackson, O., d. December 20, 1909, at Columbus, O.; m. March 15, 1893, at Jackson, O., to Susan McClure, b. February 9, 1865.

Generation VI.

Children of Harry H. and Susan (McClure) Long.

508 Harry Bertis, b. April 18, 1896, d. April 20, 1896.

Stella Marie Long (Gen. V, No. 240), b. September 1, 1868, at Jackson, O.; m. February 7, 1895, at Jack-

son, O., to Albert C. Hitchcock, b. January 10, 1870, d. September 21, 1895.

Cornelia Virginia Long (Gen. V, No. 241), b. July 3, 1875, at Jackson. O.; m. January 22, 1902, at Charleston, W. Va., to Otis A Thayer, b. July 24, 1879.

Generation VI.
Children of Otis A. and Cornelia (Long) Thayer.

509 Virginia Annette, b. November 4, 1902, at Charleston, W. Va

510 Harry James, b. March 21, 1907, at Charleston, W. Va.

511 Otis Long, b. April 18. 1910, at Charleston, W. Va.

Descendants of:

Daniel Webster (Gen. IV, No. 67), and Lucy (Gillette) Hoffman.

Authority: Family records contributed by Lucy (Gillette) Hoffman.

Florence Delano Hoffman (Gen. V, No. 242), b. February 9, 1868, at Ottawa, Kan.; m. October 14, 1897, to Frank Dudley Smith, of Muskegon, Mich.

Generation VI.
Children of Frank D. and Florence (Hoffman) Smith.

512 Dudley Hoffman, b. August 10, 1902.

Descendants of:

Douglas and Julia (Hurst) Paine (Gen. IV, No. 68.)

Elizabeth Ophelia Paine (Gen. V, No. 245), b. August 3, 1841, in Jackson county, Ohio; m. December 25, 1867, at Delaware, O, to Rev. George Cherrington, b. May 30, 1842, at Evergreen, O.; d. November 7, 1900, at Evergreen, O.

Authority: Family records contributed by Elizabeth (Paine) Cherrington, No. 245.

Elizabeth (Paine) Cherrington graduated from Ohio Wesleyan Female Seminary at Delaware, O., in June, 1865

Rev. George Cherrington was a member of Ohio M. E. conference for twenty-six years. Soldier in Union army; second lieutenant 91st O. V. I.; principal of Ewington Academy at Gallia, O.

Generation VI.

Children of George W. and Elizabeth (Paine) Cherrington.

513 William Douglas, b. and d. September 24, 1870, at Ewington, O.

514 Arthur Paine, b October 10, 1871, at Evergreen, O.

515 Wanita Grace, b. April 12, 1874, at Evergreen, O.

516 Stella Janet, b. January 16, 1876, at Letart, O., d. September 30, 1884.

517 Ernest Hurst, b. November 24, 1877, at Hamden, O.

518 Edith Clione, b January 10, 1880, in Pike county, Ohio.

519 Laura, b. and d. January 1, 1883, at Wheelersburgh, O.

Descendants of:

Rev. W. W. and Julia (Paine) Cherrington (Gen. IV, No. 68.)

Authority: Family records contributed by Elizabeth (Paine) Cherrington, No 245.

Rev. William Douglas Cherrington (Gen. V, No. 246), b. June 6, 1852; m. at Delaware, O. to Mary Barnes.

Generation VI.

Children of William and Mary (Barnes) Cherrington
520 Frank.
521 Frederic.

Charles Simpson Cherrington (Gen. V, No. 247), b December 22, 1854; unm lives at Columbus, O.

Lemuel Bundy Cherrington (Gen. V, No. 248), b. June, 1857; m. Mae Elliott.
Residence, Columbus, O.

Generation VI.

Children of Lemuel B and Mae (Elliott) Cherrington.
522 Ethel
523 Harold.
524 Helen.

Rev. Edgar Hurst Cherrington (Gen. V. No. 249), b. January 23, 1860; m. at Hartwell, O., to Stella Steele.

Generation VI.

Children of Edgar H. and Stella (Steele) Cherrington.
525 Maynard.

Lora Eleanor Cherrington (Gen. V, No. 250), b April 27, 1862, at Frankfort. O., m. Rev. B. L. McElroy, professor at Ohio Wesleyan University.
Residence, Delaware, O.

Generation VI.

Children of B. L. and Lora (Cherrington) McElroy.
526 Enid Cherrington, b. July 18, 1885, at Columbus, O., graduated at O. W. U. 1907.
527 Jean, b. August 5, 1890, at Delaware, O., graduated at O. W. U. 1911.
528 Mildred, b. December 18, 1892, at Portsmouth, O.

529 Lillian, b. January 5, 1898, at Portsmouth, O.
Descendants of:

Robert and Emily (Hurst) Doyle (Gen. IV, No. 76.)
Authority: Family records contributed by Petra (Doyle) Lloyd, No. 272.

Lucile Doyle (Gen. V, No. 270), b. October 17, 1869, at Chillicothe, O ; m. December 4, 1890, at Los Angeles, Cal., to C. E. Fowler, b. February 10, 1867, at Bartlett, O.
Residence, Seattle, Wash.

Generation VI.

Children of C. E. and Lucile (Doyle) Fowler.

530 Harold Doyle, b. September 16, 1891.

531 Louise Hobson, b. February 28, 1893.

532 Margaret Ella, b. June 5, 1895.

533 Robert Charles, b. April 28, 1898.

John H. Doyle (Gen. V. No. 271)', b. September 23, 1872, at Chillicothe, O.; m. June 10, 1902, at Piru, Cal., to Minnie A. Koon, b. July 20, 1873, at Bloomington, Ill.
Residence, South Pasadena, Cal.

Petra Doyle (Gen. V, No. 272), b. May 10, 1877, at Chillicothe, O.; m. July 10, 1900, at Los Angeles, Cal., to William F. Lloyd, b. July 10, 1875, at Caldwell, O.
Residence, Alhambra, Cal.

Generation VI.

Children of William and Petra (Doyle) Lloyd.

534 Bertha Doyle, b. February 2, 1902, at Los Angeles, Cal.

535 Marian Frazier, b. July 28, 1904, at Los Angeles, Cal.

536 Petra Jane, b. January 15, 1907, at Los Angeles, Cal.

Descendants of:

Joseph and Harriet (Rathburn) Throckmorton (Gen. IV, No. 78.)

Authority: Family records contributed by Ada M. Ervin, No. 337.

Cecilia Desire Throckmorton (Gen. V. No. 276), b. March 24, 1841. at Jackson, O . d. October 20, 1887, at Ashland, Neb ; m. September 22, 1859, at Plattsmouth, Neb, to John Parry Aughey, b January 8, 1834, at Frankfort, Ind., d. July 19, 1902, at Woodbine, Ia.

Cecilia Throckmorton taught the first school in Saunders county, Nebraska.

Generation VI.

Children of John P. and Cecilia (Throckmorton) Aughey.

537 Frances Harriett, b. July 9, 1860, d. October 15, 1861.

538 Francis Eddie, b. December 30, 1862, d. February 4, 1863.

539 John Robinson, b. November 25, 1864.

540 Florence Emmeline, b. July 19, 1867.

Roanna Maria Throckmorton (Gen. V. No. 277), b. January 30, 1843, at Jackson, O.. d. November 1, 1895 at Lincoln, Neb.: m. 1860, near Ashland, Neb., to Rev. William Kendall, b. in Illinois, d. 1885, near Zork, Neb.

Generation VI.

Children of William and Roanna (Throckmorton) Kendall.

541 Joseph Miller, b. December 31, 1861.

542 Grace Ellen, b. July 10, 1864

543 William J., b. June 6, 1867, at Chicago, Ill., unmarried.

Alonzo Wellington Throckmorton (Gen. V. No. 278), b. April 24, 1845, at Jackson, O : m. December 15, 1872, near Ashland, Neb., to America Virginia Perrine, b November 27, 1842, at Williamsburg, O.

Services· Enlisted in Company C. 1st regiment N. V. C., February 17, 1864, at Plattsmouth, Neb.; mustered out July 1, 1866, at Omaha, Neb ; taken prisoner August 24, 1864, by General Shelby, paroled near Batesville, Ark., September 1., and walked to St. Louis, arriving September 12, 1864 Mr. Throckmorton is an extensive land owner and is postmaster at Homestead, Neb.

Generation VI.

Children of Alonzo W. and America (Perrine) Throck-Morton.
    544 Arthur Laureston, b. October 19, 1873.
    545 Susanna, b March 4, 1876.
    546 Harriet Cecilia, b. October 8. 1878.
    547 Ralph Harrison, b. September 24, 1887.

Descendants of:

John (Gen. IV, No. 79) and **Minerva (Tomlinson) Rathburn.**

Authority: Family records contributed by Julia Johnson, No. 89.

Cornelia Virginia Rathburn (Gen. V, No. 282), b. January 23, 1852, at Jackson, O., d. October 23, 1903, at Delaware. O ; m June 17, 1879, at Jackson, O., to David F. Edwards. d. October 14, 1889.

Generation VI.

Children of David and Cornelia (Rathburn) Edwards.
    548 David Frank, b. July 21, 1881.

549 Marie, b. May 28, 1884.

550 Jefferson R., b. 1886.

Descendants of:

Charles B. (Gen IV, No. 82), and **Delia (Lonta) Rathburn.**

Authority: Family records contributed by Ada M. Ervin, No. 337.

Ida Rathburn (Gen. V, No. 291), b. 1858, d. July 9, 1891; m. September 20, 1883, at Cincinnati, O , to Walter Bryers.

Descendants of:

George and **Eliza (Rathburn) Lucas** (Gen. IV, No. 83.)

Authority: Family records contributed by Ada M Ervin, No. 337.

George Lucas (Gen. V. No. 292), m. Gwendolyn Simpson.

Generation VI.

Children of George and Gwendolyn (Simpson) Lucas.

551 Clifford, d. young.

552 Raymond, d. young.

553 Earl, unm.

Descendants of:

Robert and **Eliza (Lucas) Simpson** (Gen. IV, No. 83.)

Authority: Family records contributed by Ada M. Ervin, No. 337.

Fanny Simpson (Gen. V, No. 294), m. Newton Newport; six children, names unknown.

Herschel Simpson (Gen. V, No. 295), m. to———
Children of Herschel and ————— Simpson.

Generation VI.

554 Robert.

Michael Simpson (Gen. V, No. 296), m. Jeanette Spangler, deceased. No children.

Lucy Simpson (Gen. V, No. 298), m. Dr. Seiford. No children.

Descendants of:

George W. (Gen. IV, No. 84) and Mary (Ridgeway) Johnson.

Authority: Family records contributed by Adaline M. Ervin, No. 337.

Hershal V. Johnson (Gen. V, No. 299), b. March 13, 1858, at Jackson, O.; married and lives at Chillicothe, O.

Ida B. Johnson (Gen. V. No. 300), b. November 12, 1859, at Jackson, O.; m. July 17, 1894, at Chillicothe, O., to Charles Bazler, d. March 12, 1898.

Generation VI.
Children of Charles and Ida (Johnson) Bazler.

555 Seward All, b. January 17, 1896, at Chillicothe, O.

556 Oakland F., b. August 13, 1897, at Chillicothe, O.

David Todd Johnson (Gen. V, No. 301), b. September 5, 1861, at Jackson, O ; married and has several children; is a telegrapher.

Descendants of:

James and Pauline (Johnson) Chestnut (Gen. IV No. 86.)

Jeanette Louella Chestnut (Gen. V, No. 303,) b. March. 29, 1866, lives at Jackson, O. Is a graduate of the Bauer Conservatory of Music, and a talented musician.

Katherine Estella Chestnut (Gen. V. No. 304,) b. July 5, 1872, at Jackson, O., m. February 14, 1911, at Jackson, O , to John T. McCurdy.

Mrs McCurdy is a composer of music and collaborated with her sister in the production of a comic opera entitled "Polaxia."

Charles Sumner Chestnut (Gen. V. No. 305,) b. January 29, 1874, at Jackson, O ; m. June 17, 1909, at Jackson. O., to Arminta Brown.

Earl Acton Chestnut (Gen. V. No. 306,) b. January 4, 1876, at Jackson, O. Is a commercial salesman.

Descendants of :

William A. and Nancy (James) Sampson (Gen. IV, No. 94.

Authority: Family records contributed by Adaline M. Ervin, No. 337.

Ida Bell Sampson (Gen. V, No. 310), b. February 17, 1867, at California. O., d. March 9, 1893, at Thornville, Ga ; m. June 4, 1885, at New Washington, O., to C. L. Quaintance.

Generation VI.

Children of C. L. and Ida (Sampson) Quaintance

557 Dale B., b August 1, 1887, at Bucyrus, O.

558 Russell Sampson, b. December 2, 1888, at Bucyrus, O.

559 Hazel M., b. June 9, 1890, at Bucyrus, O.

560 Gladys, b. September 1892, at Bucyrus, O.

Stella Myrtle Sampson (Gen. V, No. 311), b. November 5, 1868, at California, O ; m. June 2, 1887, at Smithfield, O., to William M. Brisbin.

Generation VI.

Children of William and Stella (Sampson) Brisbin.
561 Norma, b. March 4, 1888, at Smithfield, O.
562 Helen Maud, b. March 4, 1881 at Smithfield, O.

Maud Sampson (Gen. V, No. 312), b. April 22, 1872, at Independence, O ; m. August 15, 1896, at Bucyrus, O., to Samuel Sherer.

Generation VI.

Children of Samuel and Maud (Sampson) Sherer.
563 Dwight E., b. June 22, 1897, at Bucyrus, O.
Descendants of:

Charles Curtland (Gen. IV, No. 95) and **Hannah (Currie) James.**

Authority : Family records contributed by Adaline (Miller) Erwin, No. 337.

Ripley Currie James (Gen. V, No. 313), b. September 13, 1870, at Portsmouth, O.; m. April 5, 1902, at Detroit, Mich., to Janet Dodge Mitchell, b. March 20, 1869, at Detroit, Mich.

Residence, Detroit, Mich.

Generation VI.

Children of Ripley C. and Janet (Mitchell) James.
564 Margaret Eveline, b. April 11, 1903, d. May 30, 1909.

565 Charles Currie, b. December 21, 1905.

Descendants of:

Zachariah Ragon (Gen. IV, No. 96) and **Sarah (Bennett) James.**

Authority: Family records contributed by Adaline (Miller; Ervin, No. 337.

Grace Ella James (Gen. V, No. 317), b. October 31, 1878, at Chicago, Ill ; m. July 21, 1906, at Chicago, Ill., to Danner Buehler Wierman.

Children of Danner and Grace (James) Wierman.

566 Clifton James, b. July 31, 1907.

Descendants of.

Samuel G. and Mary (James) Martin (Gen. IV, No. 97.

Authority: Family records contributed by Adaline (Miller) Ervin, No. 337.

Lena F. Martin (Gen. V, No. 321), b. July 6, 1874, at Jackson, O.; m. October 21, 1896, at Jackson, O., to Ripley C. Claar.

Descendants of:

Edward J. and Ida (James) Bannon (Gen. IV, No. 102.)

Authority: Family records contributed by Adaline M. Ervin, No. 337.

Sarah Marcella Bannon (Gen. V, No. 322),b March 16, 1885, at Jackson, O.; m. June 24, 1908, at South Webster, O., to Herman B. Campbell.

Descendants of:

Anthony and Emily (Miller) Walker (Gen. IV, No. 104.)

Authority: Family records contributed by Mary May Miller, No. 327.

Frank Edwin Walker (Gen. V, No. 323), b. May 27, 1852; m September 21. 1881, at Hamden, O., to Emma Burtenshaw.

Generation VI.

Children of Frank and Emma (Burtenshaw) Walker.

567 Myrna Lucy.

. 568 William Burtenshaw.

569 Russell Anthony.

570 C. Jay.

571 Maurice Raymond.

572 Katheryn Belle.

Mary Belle Walker (Gen. V, No. 324), b. November 27, 1853; m. May 22, 1883, to Frank T. Thornhill.

Lucy Matilda Walker (Gen. V, No. 325), b. February 3, 1859; m September 3, 1884, to Harry M. Dougherty.
Residence, Columbus, O.

Generation VI.
Children of Harry M. and Lucy (Walker) Dougherty.
573 Emily Belle.
574 Draper Mallie.

David Anthony Walker (Gen. V, No. 326), b. July 8, 1861; m. March 14, 1882, to Susan McGhee.

Generation VI.
Children of David A. and Susan (McGhee) Walker.
575 Guy.

Descendants of:

David Allen (Gen. IV, No. 107) and Lucinda (Rathburn) Miller.
Authority: Family records contributed by Mary May Miller, No. 327.

Mary May Miller (Gen. V, No. 327), b. December 11, 1867, at Logan, O., resides with her sister, Mrs. Georgia Miller Denning, at Columbus, O.

Lucinda Jane Miller (Gen. V, No. 328), b. October 29, 1869, at Logan, O.; m. September 26, 1891, to Charles M. Hansen.

Generation VI.
Children of Charles and Lucinda (Miller) Hansen.
576 Charles David, b. July 9, 1892, d. August 6, 1892, at Chicago, Ill.
577 Norma Knight, b. July 21, 1895, at Coronado Beach, Cal., d. 1899.

Georgia Miller (Gen. V, No. 329). b. October 13, 1872, at Logan. O., m. June 11, 1897, at Logan, O., to Leslie B. Denning.

Generation VI.

Children of Leslie and Georgia (Miller) Denning.

578 Dorothy, b. May 4, 1900, at Mt. Clemens, Mich., d. October 3, 1900, at Wellston, O.

579 Leslie Burk. Jr., b. June 12, 1902, at Wellston, O.

Descendants of:

Samuel H. and Maria (Miller) Books (Gen. IV, No. 108.)

Authority: Family records contributed by Mary May Miller, No. 327.

Linnie May Books (Gen. V, No. 331), b. September 11, 1855; m. February 12, 1887, to James Karshner.

Generation VI.

Children of James and Linnie (Books) Karshner.

580 Donald B., b. April 25, 1888.

Oscar E. Books (Gen. V, No. 333), b. September 14, 1859; m. 1895, at Chillicothe, O , to Clara Van Meter.

David T. Books (Gen. V, No. 334), b. February 17, 1862, died.

Samuel H. Books, Jr. (Gen. V. No 335), b. April 7, 1864; m. March 1, 1896, to Elizabeth Medert.

Frank E. Books (Gen. V, No. 336), b. March 23, 1866; m. Kate Froblet.

Generation VI.

Children of Frank E. and Kate (Froblet) Books.

581 Harry S., b. January 28, 1887.

Descendants of

Alonzo (Gen IV, No. 109), and Elizabeth (Rooke) Miller.

Authority· Family records contributed by Adaline M Ervin, No 337.

Mary Adaline Miller (Gen. V, No. 337), b. March 14, 1868, at Jackson, O.; m. June 20, 1888, at Jackson, O., to Edgar Wells Ervin, b. September 28, 1863, near Wellston, O.

Residence, Jackson, O.

Generation VI.

Children of Edgar W. and Mary Adaline (Miller) Ervin.
582 Ethel Fay, b. March 16, 1889, at Jackson, O.
583 Mary Miller, b. and d. February 12, 1893.

Emily Annette Miller (Gen. V, No. 338), b September 14, 1869, m. October 22, 1896, at Jackson, O., to Eben A. Townsley, b. May 1, 1868, near Cincinnati, O.

Generation VI.

Children of Eben R. and Emily (Miller) Townsley
584 Edna, b. March 18, 1899, at Cincinnati, O.

Bertha May Miller (Gen. V, No. 339), b. September 10, 1871, at Jackson, O.; m. October 22, 1891, at Jackson, O , to Oscar P. Schellenger, b. May 10, 1865, near Jackson, O., d. April 17, 1904.

Oscar P. Schellenger served as Jackson county deputy auditor from October 1890-1896   Elected auditor and served from 1896-1902.

Generation VI.

Children of Oscar P, and Bertha (Miller) Schellenger.
585 Infant girl, b. and d. May 16, 1893.
586 Vivian Gail, b May 14, 1894, at Jackson, O.

587 Dorothy May, b. November 11, 1895, at Jackson, O.

David Allen Miller (Gen. V, No. 340), b. March 14, 1874, at Jackson, O., m. November 6, 1899, at Jackson, O., to Amy Blanch Mason, b. May 4, 1880, at Lyra, O.

Generation VI.

Children of David A and Amy (Mason) Miller.

588 Avery Lloyd, b. August 21, 1900, at Jackson, O.

589 Elizabeth Cleo, b. March 23, 1902, at Jackson, O. .

590 David Eben, b. February 14, 1904, at Jackson, O.

591 Ruth Caroline, b. May 29, 1906, at Jackson, O.

592 Mary Pauline, b. December 12, 1908, at Jackson, O.

Caroline Bundy Miller (Gen. V, No. 341), b. March 10, 1876, at Jackson, O.; m. May 3, 1905, at Covington, Ky., to John F. Schadle.

Elizabeth Rooke Miller (Gen. V, No. 343), b. October 13, 1881, at Jackson, O.; m. January 25, 1910, at Norwood, O., to Harry R Pfister.

Elizabeth Rooke Miller is a graduate of College of Music, Cincinnati, O.

Generation VI.

Children of Harry and Elizabeth (Miller) Pfister.

593 Adalyn Louise, b. January 12, 1911.

Descendants of:

George A. and **Addie (Miller) Gold** (Gen. IV, No. 110.)

May Maria Gold (Gen. V, No. 344), b. March 31, 1869, d. September 7, 1897; m. December 12, 1888, to Alfred Dixon.

Generation VI.

Children of Alfred and May (Gold) Dixon.

594 George Alfred, b. June 3, 1891, d. January 7, 1893.

595 Leonard Gold, b. September 7, 1897, d. September 7, 1897.

Descendants of:

Lewis and Amanda (Long) Atkinson (Gen. IV, No. 111.)

Charles Andrew Atkinson (Gen. V, No. 350), b. February 9, 1852, at South Webster, O.; m. December 25, 1876, at Camba, O., to Florence Bell Gilliland, b. June 6, 1857.

Residence, Chicago, Ill.

Generation VI.

Children of Charles A. and Florence (Gilliland) Atkinson.

596 Lewis Hugh, b. February 21, 1878, at Jackson, O., d. December 26, 1893, at Lincoln, Neb.

Eliza Long Atkinson (Gen. V, No. 351), b. May 1, 1856, at Jackson, O., m. May 30, 1879, at Jackson, O. to Milton F. Strider.

Generation VI.

Children of Milton F. and Eliza (Atkinson) Strider.

597 Caroline Fischer, b. February 24, 1881, at Jackson, O.

598 Fred Coffman, b. December 5, 1882, at Cleveland, O.

599 Edith Bell, b. August 29, 1885, at Leavenworth, Kan.

600 Pauline Atkinson, b. May 22, 1887, at St. Louis, Mo.

Caroline Bundy Atkinson (Gen. V, No. 353), b. March 1, 1866, at Jackson, O., m October 23, 1889, at Jackson, O., to Charles N. Jones.

Residence, Wellston, O., and Chicago, Ill.

Descendants of:

Elias (Gen. IV, No. 112) and Emma (Carrick) Long.

Authority. Family records contributed by Adaline M. Ervin, No. 337.

Lilly Dale Long (Gen. V, No. 354), b. March 17, 1862. Is an active worker in the M. E. church and a reader of some note; lives at Jackson, O.

Eliza James Long (Gen. V, No. 355), b. December 8, 1863; m. October 9, 1881, to John Brown.

Residence, Columbus, O.

Generation VI.

Children of John and Eliza (Long) Brown.
601 George, b. September 29, 1893.

Effie Alice Long (Gen. V, No. 356), b. August 27, 1865; m. December 22, 1886, to Vance Speelman.

Generation VI.

Children of Vance and Effie (Long) Speelman.
602 Gladys Pearl, b. November 20, 1889.
603 Elias M., b. October 20, 1892, d. June 28, 1893.
604 Sanford R , b. May 5, 1894.

Amanda L. Long (Gen. V, No. 357), b September 30, 1867, at Jackson, O.; m. October 8, 1889, to Dr. Asa C. Messenger.

Residence, Xenia, O.

Mrs. Messenger graduated from Jackson high school in 1886 and wrote the first class song. Finished the art course at O. W. U., at Delaware, O., in 1889;

member of Clionian society; was hospital matron while Dr. Messenger was resident physician at O. S., and S. O. Home, at Xenia, O. For four years regent of the Catherine Green Chapter. D. A. R. at Xenia.

Generation VI.

Children of Dr Asa and Amanda (Long) Messenger.

605 Harold, b. January 10, 1891.

606 Lois, b December 9, 1895

607 Emily, b. March 15, 1898.

Andrew A. Long (Gen. V, No. 358), b. December 12, 1869, at Jackson, O , d. December 6, 1894, at Jackson, O.

Andrew Long took the commercial course at O. W. U. in 1890 and 1891. He took an active part in politics and was considered as among the coming young republicans. He met a tragic death by falling in a shaft at the New Emma coal mine with which he was connected.

Elizabeth Lena Long (Gen. V. No. 359), b. January 19, 1872, at Jackson, O.. m. February 15, 1910, at Columbus, O., to George Hubbard Taylor.

Nellie Boles Long (Gen. V, No 360), b. March 18. 1874, at Jackson, O.; m. August, 1908, to John C. Harriman.

Residence, Toledo, O.

Generation VI.

Children of John C. and Nellie (Long) Harriman.

608 John Clifford, b. June 7, 1910, at Columbus, O.

Mary Frances Long (Gen. V, No. 361), b. July 15, 1876, at Jackson. O.; m ~~1901~~ to George Edward Gilliland. 1894

Residence, Columbus, O.

Generation VI.

Children of George E. and Mary (Long) Gilliland.

609 Pauline

610 Margaret Elizabeth.

611 Edward.

612 Nellie.

Descendants of:

John James (Gen. IV. No. 113) and Sarah (McNeil) Long.

Authority: Family records contributed by C. A Long, No. 367.

Cornelia Virginia Long (Gen. V, No. 366), b. March 27, 1868, at Jackson, O.; m. October 7, 1891, at North Bend, Neb , to Rev Charles C. Wilson, b. June 6, 1862, at Oil City, Pa.

Residence, Gothenburg, Neb.

Charles A. Long (Gen. V. No. 367), b. August 8, 1870, at Jackson, O.; bookkeeper; lives at Holdredge, Neb.

Luiza E. Long (Gen. IV, No. 368), b. June 18, 1874, at Jackson, O.; m. August 3, 1893, at North Bend, Neb., to Christopher F. Kahley, b. July 28, 1871, at Gladbrook, Ia.

Generation VI.

Children of Christopher and Luiza (Long) Kahley.

613 Charles L., b. February 9, 1894, at Gladbrook, Ia.   -

614 Dunham M., b. July 22, 1897, at Gladbrook, Ia.

Descendants of:

Jacob A. (Gen. IV, No. 114), and Ella (Dascomb) Long.

Authority: Family records contributed by Adaline M. Ervin, No. 337.

Frank J. Long (Gen. V, No. 369), b. September 1, 1871, at Jackson, O.; m. October 5, 1902, in Vinton county, Ohio, to Stella Shack.

Generation VI.

Children of Frank J. and Stella (Shack) Long.

615 Helen Maxine, b. October 4, 1904, at Jackson, O.

616 Gwendolyn Frances, b. January 19, 1908, at Jackson, O.

Eliza Flora Long (Gen. V, No. 370), b. February 3, 1874, at Jackson, O.; m. December 24, 1902, at Jackson, O., to Harry Lafaber.

Generation VI.

Children of Harry and Eliza (Long) Lafaber.

617 Donald J., b October 20, 1903, at Jackson, O.

618 Harry Frank, b. July 9, 1906, at Jackson, O.

619 Ella Grace, b. June 23, 1908, at Jackson, O.

620 Margaret Catherine, b. July 23, 1910, at Jackson, O.

Descendants of:

George and Harriet (Cooke) Welles (Gen. IV, No. 115.

Authority: Family records contributed by Clara B. McCluer, No. 131.

Clara Welles (Gen. V, No. 377), b. 1832; m. Harry Crawford, of Duluth, Minn.

Generation VI.

Children of Harry and Clara (Welles) Crawford.

621 Welles.

622 Cornelia Chapin.

Descendants of:

Rathbone and Sarah (Cooke) Van Winkle (Gen. IV, No 116)

Munson Cooke Van Winkle (Gen. V, No. 378), b. February 4, 1860, d. July 28, 1906, buried at Baltimore, Md , m. Mary Schell, of Baltimore.

Henry Cooke Van Winkle (Gen. V. No. 379). b. November 2. 1862, d April 21, 1904; m. Jennie Thayer, of Parkersburg, W. Va.

Generation VI.

Children of Henry and Jennie (Thayer) Van Winkle.

623 Donna Fayvette.

Juliette Van Winkle (Gen. V. No. 380), b. August 14, 1866, m December 5, 1888, to Charles E. Morrison. b. December 17, 1865, at Parkersburg, W. Va.

Services of Charles Morrison · Commissioned captain in second regiment West Virginia national guard, May 14, 1892, and major in 1897; mustered into the U S. service as captain in the 1st regiment W. Va. V. I., May 14, 1898; mustered out with regiment, February 4, 1899; again ordered on duty as major in W. Va. N. G , and promoted colonel second infantry August 19, 1900, and still in command of his regiment on January 1, 1907.

Generation VI.

Children of Charles and Juliette (Van Winkle) Morrison.

624 Juliette Corinne, b. June 30, 1893.

625 Rozalie Zell, b. August 31, 1895.

Harriette Van Winkle (Gen. V, No. 381), b. August 6, 1868; m. September 20, 1906, to Ralph E. Finnell.

Descendants of:

Judge John and **Clara Bettie (Cook) McCluer** (Gen. IV, No. 131.

Authority: Family records contributed by Clara B. McCluer, No. 131.

James Steele McCluer (Gen. V. No. 395), b. November 15, 1877, at Parkersburg, W. Va.; m. October 21, 1903, to Birdie Burroughs Baker.

Generation VI.

Children of James S. and Birdie (Baker) McCluer.

626 Anna Elizabeth, b. August 3, 1905.

John Cameron McCluer (Gen V, No. 396), b. September 15, 1879, at Parkersburg, W. Va.; m. November 18, 1903, to Annie Laurie McKinney.

Generation VI.

Children of John C and Annie (McKinney) McCluer.

627 John Cameron, b. May 11, 1906.

Henry Randolph McCluer (Gen. V, No. 397), b. March 15, 1882, at Parkersburg, W. Va.; m. Mary Thompson.

Generation VI.

Children of Henry R. and Mary (Thompson) McCluer.

628 Julia Thompson, b. June 7, 1909.

John Grigsby McCluer (Gen. V, No. 398), b. August 11, 1884; m. Daisy Stork.

Generation VI.

Children of John G. and Daisy (Stork) McCluer.

629 Virginia Cook, b. September 8, 1906.

Descendants of:

James B. (Gen. IV, No. 143), and **Cornelia Dicka-**
son) Paine.

Fannie Elizabeth Paine (Gen. V, No. 413). b. July
9, 1881, at Hamden, O.; m. December 25, 1904, at
Jackson, O., to James Edward Newell, b. June 20, 1879,
at Bristol, Ind
. Residence, Bristol, Ind.

James Basil Paine (Gen. V, No. 414), b. August
8, 1883, at Hamden, O.; resides with his mother at
Jackson, O.

Descendants of:

Bennett R. (Gen. IV, No. 145), and **Alice (Wilcox)**
Paine.
Authority: Family records contributed by Kate
(Richmond) Paine.

Howard Shepard Paine (Gen. V, No. 415), b. May
12, 1880, at Hamden, O ; m. June 16, 1909, at Fort
Smith, Ark , to Kate Richmond, b. September 7, 1888,
at Prescott, ~~Ariz.~~ Ark.
Residence, Washington, D. C.
Howard Paine is a graduate of O. S. U., at Athens,
O.; chemist.

Descendants of:

David L (Gen. IV, No. 149) and **Emeline (Dalby)**
Hurst.
Authority: Family records contributed by J. M.
Hurst, No. 153.

Clyde W. Hurst (Gen. V, No. 421), b April 13, 1858, at Chillicothe, O.; m. November 30, 1899, at Columbus, O., to Hortense Asbaugh.

Residence, Columbus, O.

Generation VI.

Children of Clyde and Hortense (Asbaugh) Hurst.
630 Helen J.
631 Pauline.
632 Maynard.
633 Mary Louise.

Descendants of:

Wilson R. (Gen. IV, No. 151), and Ella (Patterson) Hurst.

Authority: Family records contributed by J. M. Hurst, No. 153.

Mellie Hurst (Gen. V, No. 425), b. November 1, 1870, at Piketon, O.; m September 17, 1902, at Piketon, O., to Rev. Edward R. Stafford, b. April 8, 1874.

Residence, Jackson, O.

Generation VI.

Children of Edward R. and Mellie (Hurst) Stafford.
634 Infant, d. July 31, 1903.
635 Miriam Kenyon, b. August 3, 1904.
636 Thomas II, b. December 1907, d January, 1908.
637 Willis Lincoln, b February, 8, 1909.

C. Scott Hurst (Gen. V, No. 426), b. April 5, 1873, at Piketon, O.; m. October 27, 1900, at New York city, to Frances T. Remington, b. July 28, 1879, at Jersey City.

Residence, Columbus, O.

Generation VI.

Children of C Scott and Frances (Remington) Hurst.

638 Dewitt W., b. July 27, 1901, at New York city.

639 Robert, b. February 19, 1903, d. July 3, 1903.

640 Charles S., b. July 21, 1906.

641 John A. b. February 10, 1909.

642 Frederic A , b. February 10, 1909.d. Feb. 10, 1909.

Descendants of:

Joseph M. (Gen. IV, No. 153), and **Catherine (Little) Hurst.**

Authority: Family records contributed by J. M. Hurst, No. 153

Lemuel J. Hurst (Gen. V, No. 429), b. April 14, 1871, in Ross county, O ; m. May 10, 1893, at Circleville, O., to ~~Olive Alkire~~ Mary Hoskins.

Residence, Williamsport, O.

Carl L. Hurst (Gen. V, No. 430), b. February 10, 1877, in Ross county, O., m. June 13, 1906, at Circleville, O., to Olive Alkire.

Generation VI.

Children of Carl L. and Olive (Alkire) Hurst.

643 Harry Alkire, b. August 10, 1907.

644 Mary Katheryn, b. June 7, 1909.

Elwin L. Hurst (Gen. V, No. 431), b. February 10, 1877, in Ross county, Ohio; m. September 6, 1904, at Clarksburg, O., to Bessie M. Graham, b. April 25, 1884.

Generation VI.

Children of Elwin L, and Bessie (Graham) Hurst.

645 Infant daughter, d December 4, 1909.

132

Descendants of:

Douglas (Gen. IV, No. 155,) and Laura (Morrow) Hurst.

Authority: Family records contributed by J. M. Hurst, No. 153.

Ethel M. Hurst (Gen. V, No. 432), b. June 11, 1882. in Ross county, Ohio; m November 10, 1909, to Rev. John Harrow.

Residence, Red Cape, Palma, West Africa.

Gilbert S. Hurst (Gen. V, No. 433), b. May 31, 1885, in Ross county, Ohio; m. August 31, 1909, to Cecil Parker, b. November 24, 1892.

Residence, Chillicothe, O.

Descendants of:

Charles B. (Gen. IV, No. 156), and Ella (Warner) Hurst.

Authority: Family records contributed by J. M. Hurst, No. 153.

Myrtle Hurst (Gen. V, No. 436), b. March 21, 1881, in Ross county, Ohio, m. May 8, 1901, to Rev. Charles Morrison.

Residence, Racine, O.

Roy W. Hurst (Gen. V, No. 437), b. March 11, 1886, in Ross county, Ohio; m. March 22, 1905, to Florence J. Morrison.

Generation VI.

Children of Roy W. and Florence (Morrison) Hurst.
    646 Jeanette M., b December 22, 1905.
    647 E. Corlene, b September 17, 1907.
    648 Marguerite W., b. September 19, 1909.

Descendants of:

Rev. George and Elizabeth (Paine) Cherrington (Gen. IV, No. 157.)

Authority. Family records contributed by Elizabeth (Paine) Cherrington, No. 157.

Rev. Arthur Paine Cherrington (Gen. V, No. 439), b. October 10, 1871, at Evergreen, O.; graduate of O. W. U., at Delaware, O., 1900; pastor of M. E. church at Gallipolis, O

Wanita Grace Cherrington (Gen V, No. 440), b. April 12, 1874, at Evergreen, O , d. January 18, 1909, at Columbus, O.; m. October 19, 1899. at Sedalia, O., to Elmer L. Hatcher, b. March 24, 1871, near Kingston, O.

Generation VI.

Children of Elmer L. and Wanita (Cherrington) Hatcher.

649 Paul Cherrington, b. August 21, 1900, at Kingston, O.

650 Robert James, b. August 14, 1903, at Columbus, O.

Ernest Hurst Cherrington (Gen. V, No. 442), b. November 24, 1877, at Hamden, O.; m. March 17, 1903, at Delaware, O., to Betty Clifford Denny, b. July 20, 1881, at Palestine, Texas. Editor of ''The American Issue,'' and ''The American Patriot.''

Residence, Westerville, O.

Generation VI.

Children of Ernest and Betty (Denny) Cherrington.

651 Ernest Hurst, Jr., b. September 10, 1909, at Westerville, O.

Edith Clione Cherrington (Gen. V, No. 443), b. January 10, 1880, in Pike county, Ohio.; m. October 23,

1906, at Pataskala, O , to James J. Bailey, b. November 10, 1855, at Gallipolis, O.

Residence, Gallipolis, O.

Generation VI.

Children of James J. and Edith Clione (Cherrington) Bailey.

652 Ruth Cherrington, b. March 12, 1908, at Gallipolis, O.

Descendants of:

Hon Joseph B. and Julia (Bundy) Foraker (Gen. IV, No. 159.)

Authority: Family records, contributed by Julia (Bundy) Foraker, No. 159.

Joseph Benson Foraker, Jr. (Gen. V. No. 445), b. July 23, 1872, at Cincinnati, O.

Residence, Cincinnati, O. Vice president of traction company.

Florence M. Foraker (Gen. V, No. 446), b. September 14, 1874, at Cincinnati. O.; m. November 14, 1901, at Cincinnati, O., to Randolph Matthews, b. September 19, 1874, at Cincinnati, O.

Residence, Cincinnati, O.

Generation VI.

Children or Randolph and Florence (Foraker) Matthews.

653 Foraker, b. November 28, 1902, at Cincinnati, O.

654 Mary Ann Randolph, b. April 5, 1905, at Cincinnati, O.

655 Caroline Paine, b. January 20, 1907, at Cincinnati, O.

656 Florence, b June 15, 1909, at Cincinnati, O.

657 Randolph, b. May 3, 1911, at Cincinnati, O.

Louise Foraker (Gen. V, No. 447), b. October 16, 1876, at Cincinnati, O., m November 29, 1911, at Washington, D. C., to Victor Nilssen Cushman, b. February 12, 1872, at Carondolet, Missouri.

Residence, New York and Bar Harbor, Me.

Julia Bundy Foraker (Gen. V, No. 448), b. January 31, 1880, at Cincinnati, O.; m. January 8, 1902, at Washington, D. C., to Francis King Wainwright, b. May 22, 1877. at Philadelphia, Pa.

Residence, Bryn Mawr, Pa.

Generation VI.

Children of Francis K. and Julia (Foraker) Wainwright.

658 Joesph Benson Foraker, b. January 6, 1911.

Descendants of:

Harvey and **Eliza (Bundy) Wells** (Gen. IV, No. 160.)

Authority: Family records contributed by Harry Wells, No. 450.

Harry Wells (Gen. V, No. 450), b. May 30, 1877, at Wellston, O.; m March 30, 1903, at Wellston, O., to Esther Elliott.

Residence, Wellston, O.

Descendants of:

John R. and **Mary (Shipman) Everett** (Gen. IV, No. 161.)

Authority: Family records contributed by Ella F. Bailey, No. 190.

Harriet Anna Maria Everett (Gen. V, No. 451), b. September, 1852; m. June 9, 1881, at Elmdale, Kan., to Phineas Cicero Jeffrey.

136

Generation VI.

Children of Phineas and Harriet (Everett) Jeffrey.

659 William Everett, b. November 18, 1883, d. June 15, 1887.

660 George, d. young.

Descendants of:

Joshua S. (Gen. IV, No. 162), and Sarah (Carpenter) Shipman.

Authority· Family records contributed by Ella F. Bailey, No. 190.

Charles Frederic Shipman (Gen. V, No. 453, b. July, 1857; m. February 7, 1886, to Jennie Thomas.

Generation VI.

Children of Charles F. and Jennie (Thomas) Shipman.

661 Birdie Emma.

662 Lyle.

Descendants of:

Joshua S. and Jennie (Gifford) Shipman.

Authority: Family records contributed by Ella F. Bailey, No. 190.

Julia Sloper Shipman (Gen. V, No. 454), m. December, 1888, to Claude M. Breese, son of A. M. and Hannah Breese.

Generation VI.

Children of Claude M. and Julia (Shipman) Breese.

663 Carl.

Arthur Bartlett Shipman (Gen. V, No. 455), m. February 20, 1890, at Strong City, Kan., to Estella Caumm.

Generation VI.

Children of Arthur B. and Estella (Caumm) Shipman.
    664 Myrtle.

Annie Maud Shipman (Gen. V, No. 456, m. August 23, 1883, at Cedar Point, Kan., to Louis Frye.

Descendants of:

Robert M. and Sarah (Bailey) Hunter (Gen. IV, No. 174.)

Authority: Family records contributed by Ella F. Bailey, No. 190.

Martha Aurelia Hunter (Gen. V, No. 469), b. September 15, 1860; m. James Greene.

Carrie Hunter (Gen. V, No. 470), m. October 22, 1892, at Neoga, Ill., to George W. Potts, b. in Cole county, Illinois, son of Joseph and Nancy Potts.

Generation VI.

Children of George W. and Carrie (Hunter) Potts.
    665 Lennard Hunter, b. at Decatur, Ill.
    666 Neva Lucretia, b. at Decatur, Ill.

Lucy Lorena Hunter (Gen. V, No. 472), m. December 24, 1890, at Neoga, Ill., to Frederic Buchanan, b. at Neoga, Ill., son of John and Margaret Buchanan.

Generation VI.

Children of Frederic N. and Lucy (Hunter) Buchanan.
    667 Leila Margaret, b. at Neoga, Ill.
    668 Helen Hunter, b. at Neoga, Ill.
    669 Mary Lorena, b. at Neoga, Ill.

Descendants of:

James and **Mary Annette (Bailey) Walton** (Gen. IV, No. 189.)

Authority. Family records contributed by Ella F. Bailey. No. 190.

Mary Emerson Walton (Gen. V, No. 482, b. at Lincoln, Neb , m. October, 1891, at Lincoln, Neb., to Frank W. Ferris.

Residence, Eveleth, Minn.

Generation VI.

Children of Frank W. and Mary (Walton) Ferris.

670 Esther Annette
671 Peter Francis.
672 Walton Cutler.
673 Doritha Lois.
674 Muriel Elizabeth, d. October 30, 1905.
675 Virginia, d. October 30, 1905.

Descendants of:

Lewis and **Sarah (Bailey) Boardman** (Gen. IV, No. 194.)

Authority. Family records contributed by Ella F. Bailey, No. 190.

Sarah Grace Boardman (Gen. V, No. 485, m. 1908, to Wilson Baxter.

Generation VI.

Children of Wilson and Sarah (Boardman) Baxter.

676 Bessie Inez.

CHAPTER VI.

Generations VI and VII.

Descendants of:

James F. (Gen. V. No. 227), and **Frank (Watter-house) Hoffman.**

Authority Family records contributed by James F. Hoffman, No. 227.

Ripley C. Hoffman (Gen. VI, No. 501, b. January 4, 1873, at Columbus, O.; m March 14, 1900, at Greenwood, Kan., to Josie Miles, daughter of David E. Miles. Residence, Eureka, Kan.

Generation VII.

Children of Ripley C. and Josie (Miles) Hoffman.
677 Edith Francis, b. September 27, 1901.
678 Helen, b. October 12, 1902.

Descendants of:

Rev. George and **Elizabeth (Paine). Cherrington** (Gen. V, No. 245.)

Authority: Family records contributed by Elizabeth (Paine) Cherrington, No. 245.

Rev. Arthur Paine Cherrington (Gen. VI, No. 514), b. October 10, 1871, at Evergreen, O.; graduate of O. W. U., at Delaware, O., 1900; pastor of M. E. church at Gallipolis, O.

Wanita Grace Cherrington (Gen. VI, No. 515), b. April 12, 1874, at Evergreen, O., d. January 18, 1909, at Columbus, O.; m. October 19, 1899, at Sedalia, O.,

to Elmer L. Hatcher, b. March 24, 1871, near Kingston, O.

Wanita (Cherrington) Hatcher attended Ohio Wesleyan University at Delaware, O.; was an active worker in the Methodist church.

Generation VII.

Children of Elmer L. and Wanita (Cherrington) Hatcher.

679 Paul Cherrington, b. August 21, 1900, at Kingston, O.

680 Robert James, b. August 14, 1903, at Columbus, O.

Ernest Hurst Cherrington (Gen. VI, No. 517), b November 24, 1877, at Hamden, O.; m March 17, 1903, at Delaware, O., to Betty Clifford Denny, b. July 20, 1881, at Palestine, Texas E. H. Cherrington is editor of "The American Issue" and "The American Patriot."

Residence, Westerville, O.

Generation VII.

Children of Ernest H and Betty (Denny) Hurst.

681 Ernest Hurst, Jr., b. September 10, 1909, at Westerville, O.

Edith Clione Cherrington (Gen. VI, No. 518, b. January 10, 1880, in Pike county, Ohio; m. October 23, 1906, at Pataskala, O., to James J. Bailey, b. November 10, 1855, at Gallipolis, O.

Residence, Gallipolis, O.

Generation VII. ·

Children of James J. and Edith Clione (Cherrington) Bailey.

682 Ruth Cherrington, b. March 12, 1908, at Gallipolis, O.

Descendants of:

John P. and Cecilia (Throckmorton) Aughey, (Gen. V, No. 276.)

Authority· Family records contributed by Adaline M. Ervin, No. 337.

John Robinson Aughey (Gen. VI, No. 539), b. November 25, 1864, near Ashland, Neb.; m. March 24, 1886, to Eva Elvira Butler, b. May 28, 1868, at Philipsville, Pa. Graduate of Ashland high school in 1883; of Eeslian Conservatory of Music in 1891; of John J. Mitchell college, New York, 1903.

Served five years as a band master in regular army; discharged in 1897; pensioned in 1900. Made a Master Mason in 1895, Royal Arch Mason 1904; warden three years and Worshipful Master three years; treasurer two years, now secretary. Musical director of Woodbine Normal band, 1898-1909.

Generation VII.

Children of John R. and Eva (Butler) Aughey.

683 Charlotte Cecilia. b. March 30, 1895, at Fort Mead, S. D.

684 Jerome Bertrand, b. January 28, 1897, at Fort Mead, S. D.

685 Cecil Richard, b. June 6, 1899, at Woodbine, Ia.

686 Florence Eva, b. July 5, 1908, at Woodbine, Ia.

Florence Emmeline Aughey (Gen. VI, No. 540), b. July 19, 1867, near Ashland, Neb., d. March 16, 1896, at Buffalo, N Y., m April 25, 1888, near Ashland, Neb., to Herman C. Edwards, b. September 17, 1859, in Erie county, Pa.

Generation VII.

Children of Herman C. and Florence (Aughey) Edwards

687 Lottie Cecilia, b. March 20, 1889, d. July 31, 1899; buried at Titusville, Pa.

Descendants of:

Rev. William and Roanna (Throckmorton) Kendall (Gen. V. No. 277.)

Authority: Family records contributed by Adaline M. Ervin, No. 337.

Joseph Miller Kendall (Gen. VI, No. 541), b. December 31, 1861, at Tecumseh, Neb.; m. November 23, 1892, to Minnie F. Fuchoberger, b. February 20, 1873, in Germany.

Generation VII.

Children of Joseph M. and Minnie (Fuchoberger) Kendall.

688 Joseph Floyd, b. April 1, 1894, at Lincoln, Neb.

Grace Ellen Kendall (Gen. VI, No. 542), b. July 10, 1864, at Plattsmouth, Neb.; m. August 20, 1890, at Lincoln, Neb, to Bert Meno Cole, b. April 28, 1866, at Fulton, Ill.

Generation VII.

Children of Bert M. and Grace (Kendall) Cole.

689 Clifford Bert, b. August 16, 1891, at Lincoln, Neb.

690 Earl Meno, b. February 26, 1893, at Lincoln, Neb.

691 Walter Robert, b. September 20, 1896, at Lincoln, Neb.

692 Chester Ray, b. January 12, 1899, at Lincoln, Neb.

693 Cecil Gerald, b. July 30, 1901, at San Francisco, Cal.

694 Harvey Leland, b. November 4, 1903, at San Francisco, Cal.

695 Bertina Grace, b. November 8, 1907, at San Francisco, Cal.

Descendants of:

Alonzo W. (Gen. V, No. 278), and **America (Perrine) Throckmorton.**

Authority: Family records contributed by Adaline M. Ervin, No 337.

Arthur Laureston Throckmorton (Gen. VI, No 544), b October 19, 1873, near Ashland, Neb.; m. April 30, 1901, at Loup City, to Ethel Eliza Goldsworthy, b. April 28, 1878. at Rhodder, South Wales. She is of English parentage; the possessor of a fine voice and much interested in musical affairs.

Generation VII.

Children of Arthur L. and Ethel (Goldsworthy) Throckmorton.

696 Alonzo Joseph, b. April 20, 1902, near Loup City, Neb.

697 John Raymon, b. October 8, 1903, near Loup City, Neb.

Susanna Throckmorton (Gen. VI, No. 545), b. March 4, 1876, near Ashland, Neb.; m. April 30, 1902, at Divide, Neb., to Prof. Frank H. Arnold.

Generation VII.

Children of Professor Frank and Susanna (Throckmorton) Arnold.

698 Edgar Francis, b. February 12, 1903, at Otwell, Ind.

699 Othello Worthington, b. August 19, 1904, at Otwell, Ind.

700 Mabel Gertrude, b. August 19, 1904, at Otwell, Ind.

701 Ralph Paul, b. September 24, 1906, at Otwell, Ind.

Harriet Cecilia Throckmorton (Gen. VI, No. 546), b. October 8, 1878, near Ashland, Neb ; m. April 11, 1906, at Homestead, Neb., to Murray Cornell, b. March 19, 1878. He is an agriculturist, owning a half section of land in Greely county, Nebraska.

Descendants of:

David and Cornelia (Rathburn) Edwards (Gen. V. No. 282.)

Authority: Family records contributed by Adaline M. Ervin, No. 337.

David Frank Edwards (Gen. VI, No. 548), b. July 21, 1881, in Jackson county, Ohio; m. August 30, 1906, at Columbus, O., to Edna G. Fay. Graduate of O. W. U., at Delaware, O., graduate of Harvard University; professor of economics in Boston, Mass.

Marie Edwards (Gen. VI, No. 549), b. May 28, 1884, in Jackson, O. Graduate of O. W. U.; principal of public schools at Mass, Mich.

DENISON

There is much uncertainty as to the origin of the family name. It is variously spelt Denison, Dennison, Denyson, Dennistone. It is unquestionably of ancient, and probably, of Norman origin.

In the Patronymia Britannica, is the following notice: "The Dennistowns of that ilk have an extraordinary way of accounting for their surname. One Danziel, or Daniel (say they) probably of Norman extraction, settled in Renfrewshire; and calling the estate Danzieltown, assumed therefrom the surname."

The family are unquestionably ancient; the name appearing in the Charter of King Malcom I. who died in 1165; but the Norman Danziel is probably a fiction.

The "colonial period" is to us a most interesting one, and the descendants of Captain John James and Esther Denison, are fortunate in their colonial ancestry. The name of Denison is a most distinguished one in our colonial annals, and its history begins with the anti-emigration period, for which we are indebted to the records of St. Michael's church, of Bishops Stortford, England. The writer has had the pleasure of visiting this quaint old English town, which is on the eastern border of Herts county and is thirty-two miles from London. It is also called Bishops Stratford.

The parish church of St. Michaels, a fine building with a spire, dates from the reign of Henry VI.

Bishops Stortford was in existence before the Norman conquest, and its castle, known as Waytemore Cas-

Denison.

DOMUS GRATA

Hospitable House

tle, was presented by William the Conquerer to Maurice, Bishop of London.

Sir H. Chauncey, the historian of Hertfordshire; Hoole, the translator of Tasso, and Cecil Rhodes, were natives of Bishop's Stortford.

In our ancestor, Captain George Denison and his wife, Anne Borodell, we are much interested. He is described as "a valiant young captain lately come out of the wars in England" and his conduct, both military and civil, in the early years of our country's history, thrills us with a feeling of reverence and gratitude that we are his descendants

Of his wife, Anne Borodell, we have a charming picture—and to none of our colonial grandmothers, do we turn with a more loyal or loving pride. Of such dignity of person and manner was she, that she was always designated as "Lady Ann." We are most fortunate in having a piece of her handiwork handed down to us. Family tradition says it was executed while she was a pupil in a convent in Cork, Ireland, in the year 1625.

It is now preserved in a museum at Groton, Connecticut, where the writer had the pleasure of viewing it A drawing of this wonderful old piece has been made for our book, that it may delight the eyes of many of her descendants and give them a sense of personal kinship with the ancestress whom we are so proud to acknowledge.

In the book called "The Town of Roxbury" by Francis S. Drake, he says that the family of Denison was one of distinction in our colonial annals, though long since extinct in Roxbury.

In the records of the First Church of Roxbury, page 2, we find the following:

147

"William Denison, he brought three children to N. E.—all sons—Daniel, Edward and George; Daniel married at Newtowne and was joined to the church there; he afterward removed to the church at Ipswich."

The pastor of "The First Church" was the Rev. John Eliot, afterward a famous Missionary to the Indians He came to America with William Denison in the good ship "Lion" as tutor to his sons. The name of William Denison stands third on the records of the "First Church." He was made a constable and a deputy to the general court in 1634; was a man of mark, possessed considerable property and was one of the founders of the "Free School."

With his son Edward and another Roxbury man, he was disarmed in 1637, for "subscribing to the seditious libel," or in other words, for being a follower of Ann Hutchinson—a woman who had opinions of her own upon religious subjects, and, worse than all, in the eyes of the Puritan leaders of the colony, drew the more liberal and intelligent over to her way of thinking. William Denison died in Roxbury, January 25, 1653

His wife died there February 23, 1645.

The church record of Rev. John Eliot, says of the wife of William Denison:

"It pleased God to work upon her heart and change it in her ancient years after she came to this capital, and joined to the church in the year 1632."

The eldest son of William and Margaret Denison was Daniel, who attained the rank of major general, and was highly distinguished both in civil and military affairs. He was speaker of the house of representatives, and for twenty-nine years one of the "assistants." He was born in England in 1612, and after

148

coming to America was married to Patience Dudley, daughter of Governor Thomas Dudley, and lived at Ipswich, Mass. He had two children, John, who married a daughter of Deputy Governor John Symonds, and Elizabeth, who married John Rogers, president of Harvard college.

Daniel Denison died in 1682.

Edward Denison, the second son, born in England in 1614, married Elizabeth Welde of Roxbury, and had twelve children. He lived in Roxbury where he was a man of mark. He was representative to the general court in 1652 and 1655, and was the first town clerk of Roxbury. Edward Denison died in Roxbury, April 26, 1668. His son, William, a graduate of Harvard college in 1681, died in 1718, when the name became extinct in Roxbury.

The following is an extract from a document, written by Major General Daniel Denison, December 26, 1672, to his grandchildren, John, Daniel and Martha Denison: (N. E. Hist. and Gen. Reg., 46:127.)

"Your grandfather Denison was born in England at Bishop's Stratford in Hertfordshier, in which town he married and lived till the year of our Lord 1631, with two brothers, Edward and George, who all of them had children. George the youngest brother had a son named also George, my cousin German, who was living in Stratford in the year 1672, as your uncle, Harlackenden Symounds, told me, who was that year in England, and spoke with him. My uncle, Edward, had also children, and in the year 1631, removed himself and family into Ireland, where he died and left a son called John Denison who was a soldier and major of a regiment in the time of the wars, and deputy governor of Corke, where Mr. Wainwright saw him. I

have received divers letters from him; he was living in Dublin in the year 1670. Your great-grandfather, my dear father, whose name was William, had by my dear mother, whose name was Chandler, six sons, and one daughter, two of which, viz: One son and the daughter died in their childhood; one son, who was the second named William, about 18 years of age, would needs go a soldier into Holland in the year 1624, at the famous siege of Breda when it was taken by Spinola, and Count Mansfield had an army out of England, to have raised the siege but the army miscarried, and my brother, William, was never heard of since.

"We were now but four brothers left, viz: John, Daniel, Edward and George. John and myself were bred scholars at Cambridge, where I continued till after I had taken my first degree. Your grandfather, my father, though very well seated in Stratford, hearing of the then famous transplantation to New England, unsettled himself and recalling me from Cambridge removed himself and family in the year 1631 to New England, and brought over with him myself being about 19 years of age, and my two brothers, Edward and George, leaving my eldest brother, John, behind him in England, married with a good portion, who was a minister, and lived about Pelham or in Hartfordshier, not far from Stratford, where he was born.

"My father brought with him into New England a very good estate and settled himself at Roxbury, and there lived (though somewhat weakening his estate), till the year 1653, in January, when he died, having buried my mother about eight years before."

Extracts from Parish register, Stratford, England, by H. F. Waters:

150

"The xvij of March, 1582, George Denyson, son of John, baptized."

"George, son of William Denizen, baptized 20 October, 1610."

"George Denizon, son of William and Margaret, baptized 10 December, 1620."

"William Denizen and Margaret Monck, married 7 November, 1603."

The records of St. Michael's Parish church, Bishop's Stratford, edited by J L. Glasscock, Jr., were published in 1882. By this book we find that William Dennyson was church warden in 1606 (Page 113) and George Dennyson in 1632, 1635, 1648 and 1649 (page 114.)

Mrs. Margaret Denison, the mother of Major General Denison, died at Roxbury February 3, 1645-6. Her son states that her maiden name was Chandler. Mr. Waters, finds on the Bishop's Stratford register (see above) the marriage in 1603, of William Denison to Margaret Monck. This William Denison is probably the New England emigrant. The variation in the surname of his wife may be accounted for in two ways: Mr. Denison may have been married twice, or Margaret Monck may have been a widow in 1603. William Denison, father of the general, died at Roxbury, January 25, 1653-4.

From Mr. Waters' extracts from the register of Bishop's Stratford, it would seem that the father of William Denison and grandfather of Daniel was named John. His widow seems to have married John Gace.

The history of Captain George Denison, the youngest son of William and Margaret Denison, is quite fully given in the "History of Stonington and Genealogies" by R. A. Wheeler, under the title of the "Denison Family," which with some additional

notes taken from other sources, we take the liberty of reproducing, in full:

(From "History of Stonington and Genealogies," by R. A. Wheeler—1900—pp. 334-335.)

The Denison family of New England was originally from Bishop's Stratford, Hertfordshier, England. From the old Parish register there, Stratford is spelled Stortford, and Denison is spelled in various ways: Denyson, Dennyson, Denizen, Denizon.

Generation I.

1. John Denyson, living at Stratford in 1567, d. there of plague, and was buried December 4, 1582. He m. Agnes —————, who, after his death, m. May 3, 1584, John Gace (for by his will proved in 1602, he mentions "George, Edward and William Denyson, children and my wife,") also "Elizabeth Crouch, a daughter of my wife."

Children of John and Agnes Denyson.

2. Luce, bapt. 1567, buried at Stortford, December 9, 1582.

3. William, bapt. at Stortford Feb. 3, 1571.

4. Edward, bapt. at Stortford, April 6, 1575.

5. Mary, bapt. at Stortford, April 28, 1577.

6. Elizabeth, bapt. at Stortford, Aug. 23, 1579.

7. George, bapt. at Stortford, March 17, 1582.

Generation II.

William Denison (No. 3) m. Margaret (Chandler) Monck at Stortford, England, Nov. 7, 1603. He was very well seated in Stortford or Stratford, but hearing one of the famous transplantation to New England, unsettled himself and recalling his son, Daniel from Cambridge, removed himself and family in the year 1631 to New England, and brought over with him his

son, Daniel, then aged about 19 years, and two younger brothers, Edward and George, leaving his oldest son, John, who had also been bred at Cambridge and was a minister, married, with a good portion, and who lived about Pelham or in Hartfordsheir, not far from Stratford, where they were all born. He was Vicar of Standon, County Herts, 1660 to 1670. William Denison brought with him into New England a very good estate and settled himself at Roxbury, Mass, and there lived till Jan. 25, 1653, when he died, having buried his wife about eight years before, viz.: 1645.

Children of William and Margaret Denison.

8. John, bapt. at Stratford, April 7, 1605, educated at Cambridge and became a minister, m.

9. William, bapt. at Stratford, Oct. 5, 1606, and at about the age of 18 years must needs go a soldier into Holland in the year 1624, at the famous siege of Breda, when it was taken by Spinola and Count Mansfield, who had an army out of England to raise the siege, but the army miscarried and this William was never heard of again.

10. George, bapt. at Stratford, Oct, 20, 1610, buried there 1615.

11. Daniel, bapt. at Stratford, Oct. 18, 1612, graduated at Cambridge University and went to New England in 1631.

12. Sarah, bapt. 1615, and buried at Stratford 1615.

13. Edward, bapt. at Stratford, Nov. 3, 1616; went to New England in 1631.

14. George, bapt. at Stratford, Dec. 10, 1620; went to New England in 1631.

Generation III.

George Denison (No. 14) m. about 1640 Bridget Thompson, b. Sept. 11, 1622 She was a daughter of John Thompson and wife Alice, gentleman of Preston, of Northamptonshire, England. She d. 1643. They had two children. One of whom was ancestress of Admiral George Dewey, U. S. navy.

15. Sarah, b. March 20, 1641, m. Thomas Stanton.

16 Hannah, b. May 20, 1643, m. Nathaniel Chesebrough, 1659. She m. (2nd) Joseph Saxton July 15, 1680.

This Capt. George Denison having buried his wife in the year 1643, went back to England the same year, where, as we learn from a letter of his brother, Maj-Gen. Daniel Denison. published in the April number of the New England Historical and Genealogical Register, of 1892, in which he says. "My brother, George, was a soldier there above a year; was at the battle of York, or Marston Moor, where he did good service, and was afterward taken prisoner, but got free and married a second wife, Miss Ann Borodell, who was born in England in 1615, and with her returned to New England in the year 1645, and took up his abode again in Roxbury, Mass., where he continued to live until 1651, when he came with his family to Connecticut and located himself at New London, Conn., where he resided until 1654, when he came to Stonington with his family to live, and remained there until his death, which took place at Hartford, Conn., Oct. 24, 1694.

His illness and death occurred while attending the general court. Owing to the bad condition of the roads at that time it was impossible to convey the remains to his home for burial, a distance of forty-four

miles, and he was buried in the cemetery back of the old Center church at Hartford, where his grave may be seen to-day. This ancient cemetery has been recently restored by the local chapter of Daughters of the American Revolution.

His wife, Ann Borodell, is buried in Elm Grove cemetery, Mystic, Conn.

Capt. George Denison was a member of the Congregational church of Stonington, Conn.

We learn from the records of Massachusetts and Connecticut that Capt. George Denison was not only distinguished as a civilian, but became the most distinguished soldier of Connecticut in her early settlement except Maj. John Mason. His military services are on record in our colonial archives where his eminence is recognized and portrayed. Also, you will find his name in the history of New London and Stonington, where his services are acknowledged and described in full. There is no date of the marriage of Capt. George Denison and Ann Borodell, but he was doubtless married in England. Pending their courtship an agreement was made between them, which was afterwards ratified and confirmed at Hartford, Conn., May 3, 1662, as follows: "This witnesseth that I, George Denison, of Southertown, in Connecticut, jurisdiction in New England, for and in consideration of a jointure due unto my now wife, Ann Borodell Denison, upon marriage and upon my former engagement, in consideration of the sum of three hundred pounds by me received of Mr. John Borodell, which he freely gave to my wife, his sister, Ann Borodell Denison, and I have had the use and improvement of and for, and in consideration of conjugal and dearer affection moving me, thereunto." This jointure agreement may be seen on the first Book of Connecticut state records, Hart-

ford, Conn., page 274. This recorded instrument is proof positive of the marriage of Capt. George Denison and wife, Ann Borodell, to say nothing of the births of their children and his will in his own handwriting bequeathing to them his entire property.

Another authority says that after the death of his first wife, George Denison returned to England, served under Cromwell in the Army of Parliament, won distinction, was wounded at Naseby, was nursed at the home of John Borodell by his daughter, Ann, whom he married in 1645· He returned to Roxbury, and finally settled at Stonington, where he and his wife occupied a foremost place. They were both remarkable for magnificent personal appearance and for force of mind and character. She was always called "Lady Ann." A beautiful piece of embroidery made by her in a convent at Cork, Ireland, in the year 1625, has been since her death, in the possession of her descendants; but is now placed in the museum at Groton, Conn.

Tradition says, that in those days, polishing irons were a luxury, and that, when not in use, they were considered as articles worthy of display, for which beautiful hand embroidered covers were made, and that for this purpose, was designed the exquisite piece of embroidery which is of so much interest to the descendants of "Lady Ann." While somewhat softened and faded by time, the design, showing a figure of a "young woman dressed in a flowing robe," and seated under a tree, is plainly seen. The lining of the robe is of a brilliant blue, which seems as bright as when the stitches were placed there nearly three hundred years ago by our fair ancestress. Surrounding the figure, are birds and flowers, while in the distance. rises a towered castle. "Lady Ann" died September 26, 1712, aged 97 years.

Piece of Embroidery made by Ann (Borodell) Denison, 1625

George Denison was "chosen captain" while at Roxbury, and was called "a young soldier lately came out of the wars in England." He often cammanded expeditions against the Indians, and was always most successful when commander in chief; and at one time he was provost marshal for eastern Connecticut and Rhode Island. He participated in the Narragansett swamp fight, and performed prodigies of valor.

He was captain of New London County forces in King Philip's war, with Capt John Mason, Jr., under Maj. Robert Treat, in the great swamp fight Dec. 19, 1675 Also served the next year in command of the forces raised by him as provo-marshal, who pursued the remnant of the Narragansett and Wampanaug Indians, and succeeded in defeating them and capturing the Indian chief, Canonchet, who was brought to Stonington, and on his refusal to make peace with the English was shot. He assisted as magistrate to enable the Pequot chiefs designated by the English to control the remnants of the Pequots. He was assistant and deputy from Stonington to the general court for fifteen sessions.

Captain George Denison went inland a little to build his house, but yet where he could overlook the water, and built his home in 1654, a little west of the present old Denison house, occupied now by Mr. and Mrs. Reuben Ford. This first house was built of logs. Afterward he built a larger one, called the "Mansion House," and gave it to his son, William, whose son, George, built the present one. Captain George built a palisade fort west of this house (parts of which can still be seen), where he mustered in the volunteers who met under his command in the famous swamp fight in 1676.

Services of Captain George Denison: Deputy

from Stonington to Connecticut general court, 1654, 1656, 1671, 1674, 1675, 1678, 1682-87, 1689, 1693, 1694. Captain of New London county troops in King Philip's war, 1675, 1676.

From register of Connecticut Society of Colonial Dames (1907), p. 232:

Children of Captain George and Ann (Borodell) Denison.

17. John B., b. July 14, 1646.
18. Ann, b. May 20, 1649, m. Gershom Palmer.
19. Borodell, b. in 1651, m Samuel Stanton.
20. George, b. in 1653
21. William, b. in 1655, m. widow Sarah Prentice.
22. Margaret, b. in 1657, m. James Brown, Jr.
23. Mary, b. in 1659, d. March 10, 1671.

Generation IV.

John B. Denison (No. 17), m. Phebe, daughter of Robert Lay of Saybrook, Nov. 26, 1667. He served in the Colonial Indian war. She d. 1699, aged 49 years. He d. 1698, aged 52 years.

One writer says: "It seems strange that so little should be known among his descendants, of a man so conspicuous in his time as Captain John Denison. He was the first born of Captain George Denison and his wife, Ann Borodell, and was married to Phebe Lay, Nov. 26, 1667, at the age of 21 years, after each party had been duly apportioned by their fathers in a legal contract which is recorded at Saybrook. By this deed of settlement, executed before the marriage, the respective parents conveyed 'to John Denison and Pheobe Lay, the farm granted to Captain George Denison near the mouth of Mystic river in Stonington and the house and land in Saybrook which Mr. Lay had formerly bought of John Post.' He was known as Captain John

158

Denison; held a prominent position in Stonington, and in many ways was a man of mark."

Another writer says that "John Denison lived in the old Denison house situated at the foot of Mystic Hill. It was the first house built in the village about 1669, and became a well known landmark. It always remained in the Denison family till it was taken down in 1883, and so is remembered by many yet living. Captain John Denison had nine children; six sons, one of whom died in infancy, and three daughters. All lived to be married and with a single exception had large families Large tracts of land were given to each of the sons, who were all men of influence."

Children of John and Phebe (Lay) Denison.

24. Phebe, b. 1667, d. young.
25. John, b. Jan. 1, 1669.
26. George, b. March 28, 1671.
27. Robert, b. Sept. 17, 1673.
28. William, b. April 7, 1677.
29. Daniel, b. March 28, 1680.
30. Samuel, b. Feb. 23, 1683, d. young.
31. Ann, b. Oct. 3, 1684, m. 1st Samuel Minor 2nd, Edward Denison, of Westerly, R. I.
32. Sarah, b. July 29, 1692, m. Isaac Williams.
33. Phebe, b. probably between Ann and Sarah. Phebe Denison, m Ebenezer Billings.

Generation V.

William Denison (No. 28), m. in 1698, Mary (No. 15), daughter of the first John Avery, of Groton. They lived in North Stonington, Conn.; he d. there Jan. 30, 1730. His widow, being 52 years old, was m. January 12, 1732, to Daniel Palmer, who was 59 years old. She outlived him and d. in 1762, aged 82 years.

Children of William and Mary Denison.

34. Mary, b. in 1699, d. in 1699.
35. Mary (twin), b. in 1701.
36 Phebe, (twin), b. in 1701.
37. Ann, b. in 1703, m. John Denison in 1720, and was drowned in a well in 1721.
38. William, b. in 1705.
39. Abigail, b. in 1708, m. Roger Billings.
40. Lucy, b. in 1710, m. John Swan, 2nd.
41. Avery, b. in 1712.
42. Thankful, b. in 1714, m. Joseph Billings.
43. Desire, b. in 1716, m. John Stanton.
44. Christopher, b in 1719.
45. John, b. Feb. 23, 1722, m. Martha Wheeler.

Generation VI.

William Denison (No. 38), m. 1st, Jan. 30, 1732, Hannah Burrows, who d. Jan. 1, 1737; he m. 2nd, Hannah Tyler Jan. 20, 1738, who d. in 1797, aged 86 years. He d. Jan. 29, 1760.

Children of William and Hannah (Burrows) Denison

46. William, b. Dec. 31, 1733, d. young.
47. Joseph, b. Feb. 24, 1735.
48. Hannah, b. Dec. 1, 1736, m. Dr. Charles Phelps.

Children of William and Hannah (Tyler) Denison.

49. Nathan, b. Feb. 24, 1739, d. young.
50. Daniel, b. July 20, 1740.
51. Amy, b. March 22, 1742, m. Thomas Swan.
52. Ann, b. Sept. 12, 1744, m. George Palmer.
53. Esther, b. April 23, 1746, m. John James.

Generation VII.

(From "A Record of Descendants of Captain George Denison, of Stonington, Conn., by John Denison Baldwin & William Clift. —1881—p. 90.)

Esther Denison (No. 53), b. April 23, 1746, was married to John James. April 26, 1763; lived in Preston, Conn   Her children:

54. Susanna, b. Oct. 1764.
55. Anna, b. July, 1766.
56. William, b. May, 1769.
57. John, b. June 1771.
58. Hannah, b. Dec. 1773.
59. Esther, b. 1775, d. in 1776.
60. Nabby, (Abigail), b March, 1777.
61. Polly, b. July, 1779.
62. Thomas, b. March, 1781.
63. Esther, b. June, 1783.
64. Samuel, b April, 1785.

LAY

Robert Lay, the emigrant, was the first in a line of eight Robert Lays in America, the name descending from father to son. He was born in 1617, and died July 9, 1689. He is reported at Lyme, Conn., in 1638, but settled permanently in Saybrook, 1647. Lyme is situated in New London county, Connecticut, and Saybrook in Middlesex county, the two towns separated by the Connecticut river.

The residence of Robert Lay was in that part of Saybrook, which is now the town of Essex, on the north side of what is now the street on Essex Point leading to the steamboat dock.

That street and lane was for a long time, perhaps a hundred years, called "Lays Cartpath"—and the river landing "Lays Wharf." The family homestead of that part of the family which remained in Essex, was on that spot until many years within the present century.

This Robert Lay, the first, was a large land owner, including a large tract north of Essex Point, as well as a division in the Oyster river quarter, that is, the present Westbrook In 1666 and 1678, he was a deputy to the general court In December, 1647. he married Sarah Fenner, the widow of John Tully. She came to America in 1646 or 47, with her brothers, William and Arthur Fenner, bringing with her, her son John Tully (bapt. in 1638), and a younger daughter.

Sarah (Fenner) Tully, wife of Robert Lay, died May 25, 1676, aged 59 years.

They had two children, Phebe, born Jan. 5, 1651,

d. 1699, and Robert, born March 6, 1654, d. July 1, 1738.

Phebe Lay was married Nov. 26, 1667, to John Denison (No. 17, Denison family). It is interesting to know that Saybrook was the first seat of Yale college. The following description of this typical New England village which the writer had the pleasure of visiting recently, is taken from the book entitled "In Olde Connecticut" by James Burr Todd.

"Old Saybrook is almost the only Connecticut town that boasts nobility for its founders, and a real lord and lady for its governors. Almost two hundred and fifty years ago, we learn from old chroniclers, Lord Say and Seal, Lord Brook, Colonel Fenwick, and "other gentlemen of distinction in England," procured a patent of the territory "lying west from Narragansett river, a hundred and twenty miles on the seacoast, and from thence in latitude and breadth aforesaid to the South Sea." (A quaint old document, it is said, was this patent, which, after defining in obsolete legal terms, the metes and bounds of the grant, its "privileges and appurtenances" of woods, uplands, arable lands, waters, meadows, pastures, ponds, havens, ports, waters, rivers, adjoining islands, fishings, huntings, fowlings, mines, minerals, quarries and precious stones, closed as follows:

"According to the tenour of his majestie's manor of East Greenwich, in the county of Kent in ye kingdom of England, in free and common soccage, and not in cappitu nor by Knight service; they yielding and paying therefor to our sovereign Lord and King, his heirs and successors, only the fifth part of all the Oar of Gold and Silver which from time to time, and at all times hereafter shall be gotten, had or otherwise obtained.")

The first step of the patentees was to plant a settlement in their new possessions, and early in 1635 they deputed John Winthrop, son of the famous Governor Winthrop, to build a fort on Saybrook Point, which should serve as a nucleus for the proposed settlement, and the site of which is still pointed out to the tourist, on a little eminence commanding the mouth of the Connecticut River. This fort is a central form in the history of the State. The waves of Pequot and Narragansett warfare rolled about it for almost half a century; several times it was besieged, and a hundred moving tales of ambush and rally, or capture, torture and individual murder are related by the antiquarians of the village concerning it. Only a few days after the fort was begun a Dutch vessel from New Netherlands came hither with the view of taking possession of the river, but was driven off by the guns of the fort. From its walls Captain Mason and his men on a May day in 1637 set out for the destructiton of Pequot fort and nation at Groton, and here Governor Andros in 1675 made his first attempt against the chartered rights of the colony by sailing up from New York with an armed force and demanding the surrender of the fort.

In 1639 Colonel George Fenwick arrived and continued to act as governor of the Plantation until it was sold to the colony of Connecticut in 1644, the noble owners of the patent having relinquished their former plan of improving their grant in person. Colonel Fenwick was accompanied by his wife, Lady Ann Butler, daughter of an English nobleman, the first lady of rank who appears in the colonies, and whose story forms one of the most romanic and interesting episodes in the history of Saybrook. With true wifely devotion she refused to allow her husband to depart for the New World alone, and leaving behind the comforts and re-

finements of life in the English upper class she followed him hither, and shared with him the perils of Indian warfare and privations of the wilderness. The brave lady's love and devotion cost her dear; she died in 1648, nine years after her arrival, and was buried a few yards south of the fort, on a slight eminence known to this day as Tomb Hill. The bereaved husband erected a monument to mark her grave, and soon after sailed away to England, where he figured in history as one of the judges of the unfortunate King Charles the First. For more than two hundred years the brave lady's tomb remained amid the bleakness and barrenness of the Point. At length the line of the Connecticut Valley Railroad was laid out directly through it and, yielding to the exigencies of modern progress, the interesting relic was removed. In opening the grave a floss of her bright golden hair was found perfectly preserved; it is now owned by a conductor on the Valley Railroad whose antiquarian tastes led him to appropriate that which no one else valued. The tourist now looks in the village cemetery for the poor lady's cenotaph, a shapeless monument, rudely carved from the red sandstone of the valley, and from some unexplained cause bearing no inscription whatever, probably because the hard, stern, Puritan spirit forbade to a woman the glowing panegyric necessaary in order to do justice to her virtues. This part of Saybrook is now called Fenwick, I suppose in her honor, and the large summer hotel built here in 1871 received its name, Fenwick Hall, probably for the same reason.

But Saybrook once barely missed an honor greater than those which have been narrated. Over on the south end of the Point—a region of shifting sands and bunches of beach grass, that at the touch of the sea breeze vibrates with the tune of a hundred Aeolian

harps, and which is now occupied only by the hotels and the great lighthouse—a city was once laid out, with streets and squares, a park, a public mart, and wharfs for the shipping; then the colonists began to whisper of the arrival of distinguished strangers, and to scan the distant sea line for an expected sail. The strangers thus looked for, the old chronicles go on to say, were Cromwell, Pym, Hasselrig and Hampden, the four most illustrous commoners in English annals, who at one time had made all preparations to emigrate to the New World, once actually embarking for the voyage, but were driven back by adverse winds, and from some unknown cause were led to abandon their project, and so the colonists were disappointed and the city lots left to return to their original barrenness.

It was at Saybrook that Yale College had its birth, and the first fifteen Commmencements of the institution were held there; and in this village, in the autumn of 1708, assembled the convention of Puritan ministers which adopted the famous Saybrook Platform. It may be readily imagined that the latter was one of the great events of the village.

The state of the church at that time was such as to awaken the gravest apprehensions. The liberal doctrines of Roger Williams—the most trenchant foe that Calvinism ever encountered—were advancing from the East. Antinomianism, the Anabaptist and Pedobaptist heresies were prevalent. Quakers had been harbored in the colony, and to add to the pressure of foes without there were strifes and wranglings among the churches themselves; and so the Puritan leaders called a convention of the entire church to meet at Saybrook. The delegates came on horseback from every part of the colony—from Hartford, Simsbury and the East, from Litchfield, Fairfield and the towns

and villages between. It was the season of Commencement in the college. The morning after their arival the convention met How readily the imagination recalls the scene! The throng of strangers, the pleasant air of bustle and excitement in the village, and then, at the stroke of the bell in the ancient church, grave, sober-suited figures came forth from the doors of the villagers. As in a pageant they pass down the village street On some of the faces under the broad-brimmed hats rests an almost divine benevolence, on others a grim austerity lowers, there is an earnestness and glow about them that attracts, and a severe dignity repels. How rebukingly they gaze upon the idle dreamer and scribbler under the elms! How with a look they would have crushed the petted and perfumed striplings of the modern pulpit!

The church doors close upon the retreating forms, and there is framed the platform that is to be the sheet-anchor of the Congregational churches for almost twice ahundred years.''—(By permission of the Joseph McDonough Co., of Albany, N. Y.)

AVERY

The first trace of the Groton Averys prior to the emigration to America, is found in the church at Ippleden, County Devon, England, where Christopher Avery and Margery Stevens were married.

The marriage license is dated Aug. 16, 1616.

(From History of Stonington and Genealogies.)

Generation I.

"Christopher Avery, the emigrant ancestor and progenitor of the Avery family, was born in England about 1590. He was a weaver by trade, and came to this country and located at Gloucester, Mass, where he was selectman in 1646, 1652 and 1654. At a court in Salem, he took the freeman's oath, June 29, 1692, and was chosen clerk of the band, constable and clerk of the market. His wife did not come to this country. In 1658, he sold lands at Gloucester and removed to Boston, where on the 16th of March, 1658-9 he purchased land, a small lot, about twenty-six by forty-six feet. It was located in what is now the center of the postoffice building, facing on Devonshire street. The famous old spring, which gave the name to Spring Lane, and which is now preserved under the post-office, was near. This Avery plot was a part of, or at least adjoined, the site of two notable resorts of later days—the well known restaurant whence first came the famous "Julien soup," and the "Stackpole House," not much less famous. The Winthrop estate was not far away, and nearby, in after years, Benjamin Franklin was born. Christopher Avery did not long retain his property, for March 22, 1663, he sold the land to Ambrose Dew, for forty pounds. There had

evidently been no increase of value in the five years that he had held possession. After being owned by two or three different persons, it was bought by Mr. Stackpole about 1790. Christopher Avery now followed his son, James to Connecticut, and August 8, 1665, purchased a house, orchard and lot of Robert Burrows in New London. Here he claimed exemption from watching and training, on account of age, in June, 1667, and was made freeman of the colony, October, 1669. He died March 12, 1670, by Minor diary.''

Generation II.

Many names are found in these pages, which appeal to our justifiable pride in our New England ancestry, but none more forcibly than that of the warrior-statesman Captain James Avery. His long and eventful life has been well portrayed for us. The state of Connecticut places him beside Captain Denison, and counts them both among her favorite sons. Upon the site of his homestead at Groton, Connecticut, known as the ''Hive of the Avery's,'' and for nearly three centuries a landmark of Connecticut, rises a noble monument which is visited by many beside his descendants, and to all who view it, is brought a clearer realization of the colonial history of our country, and of the part borne in it, by the man to whom this monument is dedicated. In journeying over the ancient estate of Captain Avery, mile after mile of which is rock-ribbed and stern to look upon, the writer was reminded of the character of our Puritan ancestors of New England. One portion at least of this vast estate, remains to this day in the posession of his descendants. Tradition says that it originally extended from river to river.

In strong contrast to the greater portion, this comprises many fertile acres, which seems a very ''oasis

169

in the desert " In the hospitable homestead we found
"Colonial cousins" who welcomed us and gave us of
the traditions which linger still about the land which
yet remains in the hands of lineal descendants of
Captain James Avery. A loyal and vigorous clan they
are—these Averys who have swarmed from the old
"Hive." To feel this you have only to visit Fort Griswold nearby, and hear the tales of those of Avery name
and blood, who gave of their lives and services to the
revolution in the defense of New London. Close beside it, is the "Monument House" where relics of
these valiant heroes are to be found, sacredly guarded
by the Ann Warner Bailey Chapter, Daughters of
the American Revolution. In the vault where harm
cannot reach it, is kept the beautiful old piece of
embroidery made by the fair hands of "Lady Ann"
Borodell.

Turning again to the "History of Stonington and
Genealogies," we find the following:

"Captain James Avery, the only child of Christopher, was born in 1620. Came to America with his
father, and lived at Gloucester for several years. The
Rev. Mr. Blinman, who had been the minister of Gloucester for eight years, was engaged to become the minister of the Pequot plantation. A party of his friends
proposed to move with him, and came on to make prep-
aratory arrangements, Oct. 19, 1650. It appears that
James Avery went back to Gloucester, sold his possession there to his father, and in 1651, returned to New
London. In March of that year, the principal body
of these eastern families arrived. Captain James
acquired large tracts of land at what is now Poquonoc
Bridge, Groton, east of New London. About 1636, he
built the "Hive of the Avery's" at the head of Poquo-

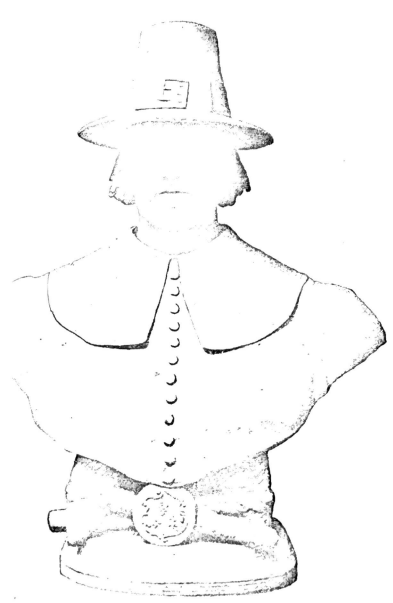

Bronze Bust of Captain James Avery,
at Avery Memorial Park, Groton, Connecticut

noc Plain, a mile and a half from the river Thames.
He was a member of the first Congregational church at
New London. In 1684 the old Blinman edifice, first
church of New London, the "unadorned church and
water tower of the wilderness," which had stood for
thirty years, was sold to Captain Avery for six pounds,
with the condition that he should remove it in one
month's time. According to tradition, the church was
taken down, its materials carried across the river, and
added to the house he had already built at Poquonoc.
In spite of this analytic and synthetic process, the
ancient dwelling seemed to have retained some of its
sacred character for two centuries later. It was occupied until July 21, 1894, when a spark from a
passing locomotive ignited its well-seasoned frame, and
in a short time only the ancient chimney remained to
mark the spot of this historic house of eastern Connecticut. A few years later the chimney was taken
down, the grounds graded, and a tasteful monument
was erected by the descendants of James Avery. He
was ensign, lieutenant and captain of the New London
companies and served through King Philip's war in
command of forty Indians from Stonington, New London and Lyme. In 1676, he was captain of one of the
four companies which protected the frontier and for
twenty-three years an officer of the town and twelve
times deputy to the general court, 1656-80; also assist-
ing judge in the prerogative court, and was most
prominent in matters relating to the church, as refer-
ences to him in such connections are numerous. He
married 1st Nov. 10, 1643, Joanna Greenslade, born
about 1622. She died after 1693. He married 2nd,
Mrs. Abigail (Ingraham) Chesebrough, widow of
Joshua Holmes, July 4, 1698. He died April 18, 1700.
His widow was living at late as 1714."

The following extract is taken from an article entitled "The Hive of the Averys," which was written by Mabel Cassine Holman, a descendant of Captain James Avery, and published in No. 2, Vol. IX, of the "Connecticut Magazine:"

"At the head of Poquonock Plain in what is now the town of Groton, Connecticut, stood for many years the house known as "The Hive of the Averys." It was built by Captain James Avery in the year 1656. This historic house never passed into strange hands, being continuously inherited from father to son, until it was destroyed by fire on the night of July 20, 1894.

Soon after the burning of this old house, "The Avery Memorial Association" was incorporated by special act of the Connecticut Legislature, received the old homestead site by deed of gift from its owner, James Denison Avery, and there erected a granite memorial in what is now known as the "Avery Memorial Park." The inscriptions on the monument briefly tell the story of "The Hive" and the names of its successive owners. The front of the die bears a bronze tablet, that gives a good representation of the old house. This tablet was the gift of John D. Rockefeller, one of the descendants. The shaft is surmounted by a bronze bust of the builder of the "Old Hive." It is of heroic size, the face shaded by the Puritan hat, showing resolution, sterness and a mighty will, while in the mouth is a suspicion of tenderness and deep feeling, mingled with strict regard for the right that made Captain James Avery, with Captain George Denison, "entreat the general court to be more merciful to the captured Pequots."

Captain James Avery, born in the year 1620, was the only child of Christopher Avery, a weaver, who was born in England about 1590. Tradition tells us he came from Salisbury, Wilts County, in the ship "Ar-

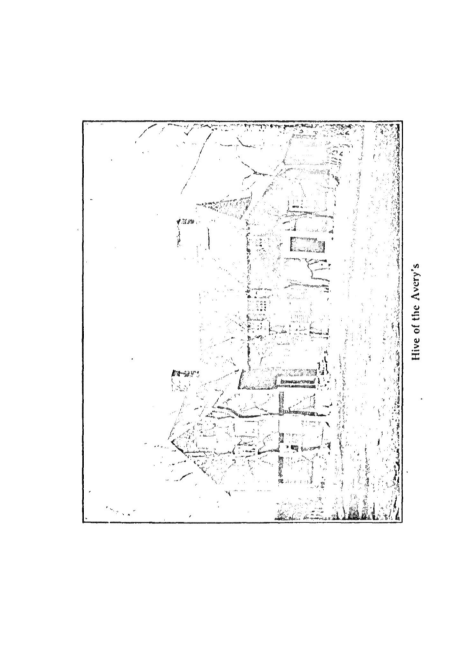

Hive of the Avery's

belle," with John Winthrop in 1630. His little son, James, ten years old, came with him and they settled in Gloucester, Massachusetts. On November 10, 1643, James Avery married, in Boston, Joanna Greenslade. We read that in the year 1650, on the 19th of October, among the grants made by the townsmen of New London, James Avery received one, said to be the land where the "Pequot House" now stands. Six years later, James Avery, with his wife and three children. crossed the Thames River and settled permanently at the head of Poquonock Plain, in the town of Groton, and there built the "Hive of the Averys" in 1656. He soon became active in military affairs. In 1665 the general court confirmed Ensign James Avery as "lieutenant to ye train-land at New London." In June. 1672. the general court ordered that Captain John Winthrop should be "chiefe" military officer for the County of New London and Lieutenant James Avery his second." In 1673 New London County was to add a hundred dragoons to her "train-bands," and for such forces as shall be called out of that county, "James Avery appoynted Captain." In 1675 knowing what Massachusetts had suffered, the name of King Philip became a terror to the Conecticut settlers, and in October the general court at Hartford put Connecticut under martial law. At the meeting of the council of the colony in the following February, "There was order to Captain George Denison and Lieutenant Minor, to rayse some forces to surprize or destroy the enemy." From the same letter we read, "The Council considering the difficulty of collecting any considerable body of the enlisted soldiers from the several townes, for an immediate march against the enemy, order that Captains Avery, Denison and Lieut Minor, should forthwith gather as many men as possible from the three nearest

towns, New London, Norwich and Stonington and taking with them the Mohegan and Pequot Indians march against the enemy." In the following August. "The Council agreed and ordered that the right and division of captives be left to the decision and determination of Captain John Mason and Captain James Avery and Daniel Witherell " In 1676 a series of forays was commenced against the Indians and were led by Captain Denison and Captain Avery There were ten of the expeditions which contributed in no small degree to the favorable results

Captain Avery was equally prominent in the civil matters of the town. He was chosen townsman in 1660 and held that office twenty years, and one of his earliest acts in this capacity shows a desire to preserve the public documents. He was twelve times deputy to the general court between 1658 and 1680 Captain James Avery was prominent in matters relating to the church. "In February 1677-78 when it was resolved in town meeting to build a new meeting house, to take the place of the old Blinman house in New London, the building committee consisted of Captain Avery and two others " In June, 1684, the old Blinman edifice, called "the unadorned church and watch-tower of the wilderness." was sold to Captain Avery for six pounds, with the condition that he remove it in one month's time. The church was taken down and carried across the river and added to the house Captain Avery had already built at Poquonock. The church record kept by Rev. Mr. Broadstreet, begins October 5. 1670, the day of his ordination with the following list· Lieutenant James Avery and wife, Thomas Minor and Wife, James Morgan, Senior, and Wife, and eighteen others."

Christopher Avery spent his last years with his son in the old house. Captain James Avery died April

18th, 1700. Such was the life of James Avery, living as he did during the early history of the country. He was a man among men and deserves the respect and confidence he received.

Not far from the site where the "Hive of the Averys" stood, lies a quiet field, far back from the village street—the old Avery burying ground. It was here Christopher Avery and his son, Captain Avery, were said to have been buried."

From a chapter on "Groton and Mystic" in a book entitled "In Olde Conneticut," by Charles Burr Todd, we have a glimpse of the old house that has earned the quaint title of "The Hive of the Averys."

GROTON AND MYSTIC.

"Groton Bank, Groton Centre, Popuonnock, Noank, West Mystic, Mystic, Head of Mystic, Fort Hill, Pequot Hill, Porter's Rocks—all are localities more or less notable in the town of Groton, which lies across the Thames from New London, and covers a territory nearly eight square miles. It is a land of breezy ridges and sunny valleys, with stern precipitous granite ledges facing the sound and walling in the valleys, a region almost undiscovered by the tourist, but well worthy of his attention, as much for its natural beauty as for its historical interest. Originally it was a part of New London, known locally as the "east side," but its inhabitants in 1705 succeeded in inducing the general court to incorporate them as a separate town, which they named Groton in honor of Governor Winthrop's English home in Suffolk County.

Our first expedition into Groton was in search of the town records, to our surprise and pleasure we found them lodged in one of the oldest houses in

America, and one which is perhaps the best specimen of colonial architecture extant. It is known as the old Avery mansion, and was built in 1656 by Judge James Avery, one of the original settlers of Groton It is a house of character. Even the casual passer-by notices it, and wishes to stop and inquire as to its history. It is ballasted by two heavy stone chimneys, its frame is of white oak, heavy enough to furnish forth two modern houses, its roofs are high and steep, the upper story projecting over the lower as in the block-houses of colonial Indian warfare. In two large safes in the front parlor the town records are kept. This parlor is a study. Its ceiling is low, and in the center is a huge beam, whitewashed, and still bearing the marks of the hewer's broad ax. The sills—8x8 beams—are placed above the flooring, and are as sound in appearance as when laid more than two hundred and thirty years ago. The present owner is the ninth Avery to whom the old house has descended from eldest son to eldest son, with the broad green fields adjoining. We found the aged Town Clerk, Mr. James Avery, busy transcribing the generations that had swarmed from the old hive for a genealogy of the Averys now being compiled in Rochester, New York.

If these old white-oak timbers could speak, we should hear about the funeral of the first James Avery in 1681, who, having been a magistrate on the bench and representative to the General Court, was buried suitably to his rank. We should have details of the grand funeral—the name of the person "appointed to look to the burning of the wine and beating of the cider for the occasion"—of the gallons of wine, the barrels of cider, the hundredweights of sugar, the gloves and gold rings furnished the pallbearers, and the white kid gloves for the attending ministers. For

a funeral cost something in those days—often as much as £200.

In 1718 the old house saw the first innovation of moment Tea was brought over from the settlement at New London, and passed from hand to hand as the family and a few neighbors sat around the capacious fireplace. Madame Avery was skilled in all manner of cooking, but she admited that she knew not how to prepare this bitter herb for the table. At last the council decided that it should be cooked and served with boiled pork, as greens; but there were many wry faces when the dish came to be eaten. At last they learned to steep it, as they did their boneset and other medicine herbs, and to disguise it with milk and sugar, but it was months before the family came to enjoy the strange beverage. Two years later they had their first sight of wheat flour; rye and Indian corn having been before that the staple breadstuffs. Then, in 1730, they were thrown into spasms of curiosity at seeing a horse and wagon driven up the lawn. Hitherto the only means of locomotion had been on horseback, the lady sitting behind her cavalier on a pillion, with her arms around his waist. A little later, in 1733, the family gathered at the breakfast table, and inspected tasted and passed judgment upon two or three Irish potatoes which had been raised in the garden in beds, much as we now raise carrots and beets. In 1734 the old timbers might have lost their identity by being smothered in paint, which that year was used for the first time in this country; as a matter of fact, however, the old house waited a century longer before receiving its first coat of paint. In 1740 the first sleigh drove up to the door, and the Avery boys and girls, of whom always there was a houseful, tumbled in for their first sleigh ride. By and by war came, and the

12   177

Averys that had gone out from the old hive made a good showing in the ranks. The thunder of the guns on the day Fort Griswold was defended was plainly heard here, and in the afternoon a breathless horseman came riding up with news—nine Averys had been killed in defense of the fort and many more wounded, among the latter Col. Parke Avery, then living in the old house; and very soon a long line of wagons came over the hill, bearing the wounded to be tenderly nursed back to health and vigor by the patriotic women of the homestead It was in 1783 that the first wall paper made its appearance, and years after that before its white and sanded floors were made acquainted with carpets. The old house has recently had a very narrow escape from destruction, for the new line of the New York, Providence and Boston Railroad, now building to connect with the new bridge across the Thames, passes within a few feet of its western gable, and had not the engineers deflected their line a trifle, would have passed through it. It is a pity that none of the old family furniture has been preserved. "My mother had fourteen children," said Mr. Avery, speaking of this matter, "and every time they came to visit me they would take away some article of furniture, saying that if they gave me the old house, they must have the furniture—so it is all gone."— (By permission of the Joseph McDonough Co., of Albany, N.Y.

Eleven years ago the following engraved invitations were issued:

"Your presence is requested at the dedication of the Avery Memorial at Poquonock Bridge, town of Groton, County of New London, Connecticut, Friday afternoon, July twentieth, nineteen hundred."

At that time this beautiful poem was read to the

500 members of the Avery clan assembled. The Memorial Association of the Groten Averys hold annual meetings in Memorial park.

President, Hon. Elroy M. Avery. Ph., D. LL. D., of Cleveland, O.

Secretary, Miss Helen Avery, of New London, Conn.

Memorial Park is the site of the "Old Hive of the Averys," a mound over which classic ivies have been entwined.

The outlines of the old house have been preserved and the front door steps have been kept intact in their original position.

THE AVERY MEMORIAL.

BY MARY L. BOLLES BRANCH

Here once an ancient homestead stood
  Gray with long years of fashion old,
From stately oak, from hallowed wood,
Were hewn its beams, and strong and good
  Uprose its walls, a race to hold

Here round the hearth sat sires and sons,
  Mothers and babes, a charming throng;
Eight times renewed the long line runs,
The youths became the aged ones,
  The children grew to manhood strong.

Honor and virtue here held sway,
  And courage high in word and deed,
Forth went the statesman on his way,
Forth marched the soldier to his fray,
  A sturdy race from sturdy seed.

Gone are the walls that stood so long,
  Mossed roof and chimney, all are gone,
  Where sheltered happy lives were passed,
Now blows at will the winter blast.
  There is no home, the spot is lone

179

Yet stay, what wonders love hath wrought!
  Here is the hearthstone of a race,
The threshold that their feet have sought,
Here to our view the bounds are brought,
  And ivies the old chimneys grace

Oh! rooms unseen by mortal eyes,
  Wherein may move the friendly guest,
Oh' walls invisible that rise
With household gods in unknown guise,
  What is there to meet our quest?

Behold, the vanished home uprears
  This granite shaft whereon to-day
Wrought in enduring bronze appears
One who shall greet the coming years,
  Chief of his race, who seems to say:

Here once an ancient homestead stood,
  Gray with long years, of fashion old,
From stately oak, from hallowed wood
Were hewn its beams. and strong and good
  Uprose its walls, a race to hold.

New London, Conn

The First Church of Christ on Groton Heights, have recently erected a fine stone edifice in which a memorial window costing two thousand dollars has been placed to the "Founder of the Groton Averys."

Dr. Elroy M. Avery, of Cleveland, O., the latest historian of the Groton Averys, will publish in his genealogy of that family now in preparation, a picture of the church at Ippieden, Devonshire, England, where Christopher Avery and Margery Stevens were married. It will contain also several Avery coat of arms.

Services of Captain James Avery: Deputy from New London to Conneticut general court, 1659-1661, 1664, 1665, 1667, 1667-1669, 1675-1678, 1680, 1682-1686, 1689, 1690, 1694, 1695. Captain of New London, fort 1673. Captain in King Philip's war, 1675. (Soldiers of

King Philip's war (Bodge,) p. 467.) Captain of Trainband of New London, May, 1681.

(From Register of Conneticut Society of Colonial Dames of America, p. 212.)

·Children of Captain James and Joanna (Greenslade) Avery.

3. Hannah, b. at Gloucester, Oct. 11, 1644, m. Ephriam Miner, June 20, 1666.

4. James, b. at Gloucester, Dec. 15, 1646, m. Deborah Sterling, or Stallyon, Feb. 18, 1669.

5. Mary, b. Feb. 19, 1648, m. Joseph Miner, Oct. 28, 1668.

6. Thomas, b May 6, 1651, m. Hannah Miner, Oct. 22, 1677.

7. John, b. Feb. 10, 1654, m. Abigail Chesebrough, (No. 4, Chesebrough family.)

8. Rebecca, b. Oct. 6, 1656, m. William Potts, of New Castle, England, Aug. 5, 1678.

9. Jonathan, b. Jan. 5, 1658, buried Sept. 15, 1661.

10. Christopher, b. April 30, 1661, d. Dec. 8, 1683.

11. Samuel, b. Aug. 16, 1664, m. Susannah Palmes, daughter of Wiliam Palmes and Ann Humphrey, Oct. 25, 1686, of Swanzey, Mass. He was a large farmer, and was chosen moderator upon the legal organization of the town of Groton in 1704, and its first townsman at the first town meeting in 1705, and held that office until his death. May 1, 1723. His farm was in what is now South Groton. He is buried about a mile northwest of Seth Williams' farm in Ledyard, on the farm of C. H. Stanton.

12. Joanna, b. in 1669.

Generation III.

John Avery (No. 7), m. Abigail Chesebrough (No. 4, Chesebrough family), Nov. 29, 1675 He owned

land in Stonington, Groton and Preston, and was in King Philip's war

Services of John Avery: Captain of the Trainband in New London on the east side of the river, 1697.

(From Register of Connecticut Society of Colonial Dames of America, p. 212.)

Children of John and Abigail (Chesebrough) Avery.

13. Abigail, b. Jan. 15, 1677, d. young.

14. Abigail, b. Jan. 18, 1679, m. James Packer

15. Mary, b. Nov 14, 1680, m. William Denison, (No. 28, Denison family). She m. 2nd, Daniel Palmer.

16. John, Jr., b. April 1, 1683, m. Sarah Denison in 1705.

17. Benjamin, b 1686, m. Sarah Denison.

18. William, b. 1687, m. Annie Richardson; 2nd Sarah Walker.

19. Anne, b. 1692, m. William Satterlee, Sept. 6, 1711.

20. Elisha, b. 1694, m. Elizabeth Babcock.

21. Desire, b. (twin), 1694.

22. Josiah, b. 1697, m. Miss Edmund.

23. Daniel, b. Nov. 1699.

24. Nathaniel, b. 1701, m. Abigail————————

25. Thomas, b. 1703.

CHESEBROUGH

The first record we have of the Chesebrough family is as follows:

William Chesebrough, b. in Boston, England, 1594, married Dec. 6. 1620, to Anna Stevenson, daughter of Peter Stevenson, by the "Blessed John Cotton," in St. Botolph's church, Boston, Lincolnshire, England.

William and Anna (Stevenson) Chesebrough had thirteen children, the sixth of whom was Samuel, baptized in Boston, England, April 1, 1627.

The death of William Chesebrough occurred on June 9, 1667, at Stonington, Conn.

The names of William and Anna Chesebrough appear as Nos. 44 and 45 on the roll of original members of the First Church of Boston, Mass.

The ancient Congregational Church, the first in the metropolis, was regularly imbodied at Charlestown the 27th day of August, 1630, and Rev. John Wilson installed as teacher. Some time in the month of August, 1632, the Congregation of Boston and Charlestown began to build the first meeting-house. The site was on the south side of State St. in Boston. The church in Charlestown became a distinct body on the 2nd of November, 1632, withdrawing from the parent church about one-fourth of the congregation. The second meeting house was erected in 1639, on Washington St., and was destroyed in the great fire of 1711.

The Unitarian movement in the United States was developed chiefly in New England about the beginning of the nineteenth century under the lead of Dr. Channing. Many of the oldest Congregational Churches

183

in New England passed under Unitarian control and
the "American Unitarian Association" was formed in
1825 This was the fortune of the First Church of Boston which is today of the Unitarian denomination The
fifth house of worship, a fine structure, was built in
1868, corner of Berkeley and Marlborough Sts.

(From R. A. Wheeler's History of Stonington and
Genealogies.)

William Chesebrough (No 1), the first white man
who made what is now Stonington, in Conneticut, his
permanent place of abode, was born in Boston, Lincolnshire, England, in the year 1594, where he married
Anna Stevenson, Dec. 6, 1620 He was a gunsmith,
and worked at his trade in England, and in this country, until he came to Stonington in 1649, when he
changed his occupation to that of farming and stock
raising, occupying and improving the large grants of
land given him by the town of Pequot, now New London.

In the early part of the year 1630, he joined a
large party of imigrants who came with John Winthrop, Esq, to this country. Mr. Chesebrough located
himself in Boston, Mass., and soon after became a member of the First Church. He was admitted a freeman
of the Massachusetts colony in May, 1631, and afterwards took an active part in public affairs. In 1632,
Mr. Chesebrough was elected as "one of two" from
Boston to unite with two from every plantation to
confer with the court about raising a public stock,
and "Prince" in his "Annals" says that this seems
to pave the way for a house of representatives in
the general court.

In 1634, Mr. Chesebrough was elected constable
of Boston, where he continued to reside for several

years Previous to 1640, he removed to Braintree, and that year was elected deputy to the Massachusetts general court. Soon after which, he removed his residence to Rehoboth, Plymouth colony, where in 1643, his list was returned at £450. The next year lots were drawn for a division of the woodland near the town, and Mr. Chesebrough received lot No. 4. During this year the planters of Rehoboth drew up and signed a compact by which they agreed to be governed by nine persons, "according to law and equity until we shall subject ourselves jointly to some other government." Mr. Chesebrough was a party to that transaction, which was participated in by thirty of the planters of the new settlement. He had taken an active and prominent part in organizing the town of Rehoboth, and at a public meeting held July 12, 1644, his services were secognized by the town in ordering that he "should have division in all lands of Seakunk, for one hundred and fifty-three pounds, besides what he is to have for his own proportion, and that in way of consideration for the pains and charges he hath been at for setting off this plantation." He was propounded for freeman at the general court in Plymouth in 1645. but was not admitted till 1648. Notwithstanding the prominent part he acted in establishing the plantation of Rehoboth, and the recognition of his services by the new town, he was not treated with much favor by the general court of that colony, which ordered him to be arrested for an affray with an Indian by the name of Vassamequine, and harshly treated him in other respects. This led him to look further for a permanent place of abode. About this time Mr. John Winthrop, Jr., acting under a commission from the Massachusetts general court, commenced a settlement at Nameaug, afterward called Pequot, and then New

London. Mr. Chesebrough visited the place in 1645, for the purpose of making it his future home. He was kindly treated by Mr. Winthrop, and urged to settle there; but finding the place in several respects unsuitable to his expectations, he concluded not to stay. Subsequently he examined the Pawcatuck region, and finally concluded to settle at the head of Wequetequock Cove He shared the friendship of Roger Williams, and was encouraged and assisted by him in removing his habitation to Pawcatuck. He did not, however, immediately remove his family there, and not until he had provided for them a comfortable place of abode. It was during the summer of 1649 that his family came to Wequetequock and occupied their new house in the wilderness. The marsh land bordering on Wequetequock Cove furnished hay for his stock in abundance.

(Page 291.)

Mr. Chesebrough was a man of more than ordinary ability and held positions of trust not only in the Massachusetts colony, but was prominent in the settlement of the town of Rehoboth, in Plymouth colony. After his place at Wequetequock was included in the township of Pequot, he was elected deputy thereof to the general court at Hartford in 1653-4-5-6, and on one occasion rate maker or assessor.

When in 1658, the Massachusetts general court asserted jurisdiction over this town, Mr. Chesebrough with others were appointed to manage the prudential affairs thereof, and one of the commissioners to end small causes and deal in criminal matters. He held the office of townsman (selectman) until Southertown was annexed to Conneticut, and was the first man elected deputy after the reunion, 1653-55-57-64, and succeeded in restoring amicable relations with the court

which had been seriously disturbed by the jurisdictional controversy. After his return he was elected first selectman of the town, and re-elected every year up to the time of his death, which took place June 9, 1667. His dwelling house stood on the west side of Wequetequock Cove, near the head of tide water.

Generation II.

Samuel Chesebrough (No. 2), the sixth child of William and Anna (Stevenson) Chesebrough, was baptized April, 1627, in Boston, England. He was married Nov. 30, 1655, to Abigail Ingraham and was buried July 31, 1673, at Stonington, Conn. Samuel and Abigail (Ingraham) Chesebrough had seven children. Samuel Chesebrough lived in Boston, Braintree and Rehoboth, Mass. He was made a freeman of Connecticut in 1657; signed the Pawcatuck Articles of Association in 1658.

Services of Samuel Chesebrough: Deputy to the general court, May 11, 1665. (Colonial Records of Connecticut, Vol. 2, p. 14.) Deputy to the general court at Hartford, Conn., May 10, 1666; July 26, 1666; Oct. 11, 1666. (Colonial Records of Connecticut, Vol. 2. p. 31.) Deputy to the general court at Hartford, Conn., May 12, 1670, (Records of Connecticut, Vol. 2, p. 127.) Deputy to general court at Hartford, May 11, 1671. (Records of Connecticut, Vo. 2, p. 147.) Deputy to general court May 9, 1672. (Records of Connecticut Vol. 2, p. 170.) Deputy to general court May 8, 1673. (Records of Connecticut, Vo. 2, p. 192.)

Generation III.

Children of Samuel and Abigail (Ingraham) Chesebrough.
3. Abigail, b. Sept. 30, 1656.
4. Maria, b. Feb. 26, 1658, d. Sept. 40, 1669.

5. Samuel, b. Nov. 20, 1660, m. Mary Ingraham.

6. William, b. April 8, 1662, m. Mary Mc-Dowell.

7 Sarah, b. Aug. 24, 1663, m. John Bolton.

8. Elisha, b. Aug. 4, 1667, m. Mary Minor, Rebecca Mason.

9. Elizabeth, b. Aug. 6, 1669, m. William Ingraham, of Bristol, R. I.

Abigail Chesebrough (No. 3), m. John Avery No. 7, Avery family.) Her mother, Abigail (Ingraham) Chesebrough, married 2nd, Joshua Holmes; 3rd, Captain James Avery, the father of John Avery.

TYLER

(From official report of the first American Tyler family reunion, at Andover, Mass, 1896, by W.

I. Tyler Brigham.)

From time immemorial there have been in various parts of Great Britain, families bearing the name of Tyler, spelled in a dozen different ways.

In Burkes Armony are recorded no less than eight Tyler coats of arms. Of those lines having descendants known to have figured conspicuously in the history of our country, are the following:

Job Tyler, Andover, Mass.

Captain John Tyler, Boston.

Tyler families of Branford and Wallingford, Conn.

The Virginia and Maryland Tyler families.

1. Job Tyler was born in England about 1621, and died at Andover, Mass , about 1700.

His descendants are seemingly most numerous of all, with corresponding number upon the roll of honor. His vitality descended to his sons, of whom he had four—Moses, Hopestill, John and Samuel

2. Hopestill Tyler, b 1645, lived to be eighty-eight. He removed to Preston, Conn , where some of his descendants made distinguished history. He married Mary Lovett, Jan. 20, 1667, and had ten children, the seventh of whom was James.

3. James Tyler, son of Hopestill and Mary (Lovett) Tyler, was born Dec. 28, 1683, and married Hannah Safford, Oct. 8, 1705. They had six children—Moses, James, Hannah, Samuel, Joseph and John. John

189

was later known as General Tyler of Revolutionary fame.

4. Hannah Tyler, daughter of James and Hannah (Safford) Tyler, born Oct. 9, 1711, married William Denison, of Stonington, Jan. 30, 1738.(See Denison family No. 38.)

From History of New London county:

"Hopestill Tyler, an aged man, died in 1733. He left a wife, Mary, and four children, viz: Hannah Buswell, Daniel, James and Hopestill. Estate, 813 pounds, sterling.

In the inventory of his wardrobe is a "close bodied coat, valued at 4 pounds, 5 shillings; a beaver hat, an orange colored cloak and a muff."

Preston, Conn, an old Tyler town, has recently published the proceedings of the bicentennial (1698-1898), of its First Congregational church. Among the statistics are found numerous Tyler entries including brief sketches of Hopestill Tyler and Rev. Samuel Tyler.

A complete genealogy of the descendants of Job Tyler is now in process of preparation.

Corrections

Page 45.   Harriet Cook, d. October 30, 1823.

Page 55.   Paul Cooke, m. December 21, 1831.

Pages 56 and 86   Frances V. Cooke, b. September 4, 1842.

Page 76.   Thomas Denison James, m April 5, 1870.

Pages 94 and 131.   Clyde W. Hurst, b April 3, 1858.

Page 100   Charles Robert Hunter, b March 5, 1864.

Page 101.   John Worthington Bailey, m November, 1870.
            Residence, Rich Hill, Mo.

Page 102   James Pennock Walton

Page 107.   John L. Kibbee, b. January 25, 1862.

Page 107.   Harry Hoffman Long, b March 17, 1866.

Page 117.   Helen Maud Brisbin, b. March 4, 1891.

Page 119.   Harry M. Daugherty.

Page 122.   Avery Floyd Miller.

Page 140.   Ripley C. Hoffman, m in Greenwood Co., Kan.

Page 141.   Children of Ernest and Betty (Denny) Cher-
            rington.

Page 181.   Johnathan Miner, buried September 15, 1681.

Page 187.   Maria Chesebrough, d September 30, 1664

Omissions

Page 44. Hannah James, m. January 1, 1806, to Bennett Cook.

Page 101 Nellie Hunter (Gen. V, No. 473), m. October 29, 1891, at Neoga, Illinois, to Jacob William McClean, b. at New Washington, Ind.
Residence, Neoga, Ill.

Generation VI.

Children of Jacob and Nellie (Hunter) McClean
Frank Hunter, b. at Neoga, Ill.
Lena Ethel, b. at Neoga, Ill.
Leon Vernon, b. at Neoga, Ill.

Page 73. Rev. Truman Simpson Cowden, b. May 11, 1827, at Gustavus, Trumbul Co., O., d. January 17, 1895, at Troy, Ohio.

Page 117. Maud (Sampson) Sherer, d September 2, 1899, at Bucyrus, O.

Page 131. Hortense (Asbaugh) Hurst. b. Nov. 15, 1873.

Page 133 Martha Hurst, daughter of Gilbert and Cecil (Parker) Hurst, b. July 18, 1910, in Ross Co., Ohio.

Page 145. Murray Cornell, b. at Streator, Ill.

Page 126. Pauline Gilliland, b. March 31, 1895.

Page 126. Margaret E. Gilliand, b. March 1, 1897.

Page 126. Geo Edward Gilliland, b. Sept. 25, 1899.

Page 126. Nelle Gilliland, b. Dec. 7, 1907.

INDEX

Abernathy,
  John, 71

Alkire,
  Olive, 132.

Allen,
  Francis W., 92.

Amiss,
  Anne Adelaide, 86
  Bettie, 86.
  Henry, 85, 86
  Maria (Cooke), 86
  Sarah Van Winkle, 86

Anderson,
  Jennie, 101.
  Marcus, 101.

Arnold,
  Edgar Francis, 144
  Mabel Gertrude, 145
  Othello Worthington, 145.
  Prof. Frank H., 144.
  Ralph Paul, 145.
  Susanna (Throckmorton), 144.

Asbaugh,
  Hortense, 131.

Athey,
  Bertha Adelaide, 99
  John O., 99.
  Martin Van Buren, 99.
  Mary (Bailey), 99.
  William, 99.

Atkinson,
  Amanda (Long), 83, 123
  Caroline Bundy, 83, 124
  Charles Andrew, 83, 123
  Eliza Long, 83, 123
  Florence (Gilliland), 123
  Rev. Lewis Allen, 83, 123
  Lewis Hugh, 123
  Mary, 83.

Aughey,
  Cecilia (Throckmorton), 112, 142.

Cecil Richard, 142.
Charlotte Cecilia, 142
Eva (Butler) 142
Florence Emmeline, 112, 142
Florence Eva 142.
Frances Harriett, 112
Francis Eddie, 112.
Jerome Bertrand 142
John Parry, 112, 142.
John Robinson, 112, 142.

Austin,
  Major, 29.

Avery,
  Abigail, 182
  Abigail (Chesebrough), 182
  Anne, 182.
  Benjamin, 182
  Christopher, 168, 169, 170, 172, 174, 175, 180, 181.
  Daniel, 182
  Desire, 182
  Elisha, 182
  Hon. Elroy M., 179, 180.
  Hannah, 181.
  Helen, 179.
  James, 176, 178, 181.
  Capt. James, 8, 9, 10, 169, 170, 171, 172, 173, 174, 175, 176, 180, 181, 188.
  James Denison, 172
  Joanna, 181.
  Joanna (Greenslade), 181
  John, 159, 181, 182, 188
  John, Jr., 182.
  Jonathan, 181.
  Josiah, 182.
  Mary, 10, 159, 181, 182
  Nathaniel, 182
  Col. Parke, 178.
  Rebecca, 181
  Samuel, 181.
  Thomas, 181, 182.
  William, 182.

Babcock,
  Elizabeth, 182.

Bagby,
  J. R., 91.

Bailey,

Alice Rosetta, 61. 100
Anna (James), 41. 49
Augustus Stone 48. 63, 104.
Bennett Augustus, 62, 102.
Bennett Augustus, Jr., 102
Bennett Cook, 48, 62, 101
Bertha, 101.
Bessie, 64, 105
Caleb, 41. 49
Charles, 49
Charles Charman 61
Charles Emerson, 62, 102.
Charles P., 41, 49. 64, 105.
Charles Pease, 48, 61.
Clara Katherine, 63, 104
Deborah (Packard), 46
Dorothy, 103
Edith Chone (Cherrington),
  135, 141.
Eliza Alberta 63. 103
Elizabeth, 47, 49
Elizabeth Burgess, 61
Elizabeth (Davidson), 102.
Elizabeth (Emerson), 62,
  102.
Elizabeth (Harwood), 49, 64
Ellen Frances 62, 102
Emerson Dudley, 102.
Emma, 41, 63, 104.
Fanny (Dickey), 62, 101.
Gassaway, 49
Georgette Elizabeth, 61
George Howard, 63, 103
George Howard, Jr, 104
George Washington, 48, 63,
  103
Harriet Dickey, 62
Helen Elizabeth, 103.
Henry, 49.
Isabella, 60.
James, 49, 64, 105.
James Dickey, 62
James J., 135, 141.
John, 101.
John A., 41, 49.
John James, 48, 61, 100.
John Worthington, 61, 101.
Julia Augusta, 61, 100
Julia (Johnson), 63, 104.
Kitty, 49.
Laura (De Vaughn), 64, 105
Lissa, 103.

Lissa (Bailey), 103.
Lizzie (Campbell), 105
Louise (Carpenter), 101.
Lucy Denison, 62
Lydia Jane, 60, 99
Mabel, 101
Maria, 47, 66
Mary, 60, 99
Mary Annette 62 101, 102
Mary (Chapman) 61, 100
Mary Elizabeth. 62.
Mary (Horne), 102.
Mary (Scott), 60. 99
Mary (Ward) 62 102
Minnie Maud 63.
Nancy, 41, 49 64, 65.
Nancy Ann, 60, 99
Polly, 41.
Polly (James), 46, 47, 59
Ruth Cherrington, 135, 141
Sally, 41.
Sarah, 61, 100   - ‿
Sarah Bertha, 63, 103.
Sarah Elizabeth 60
Sarah (McClure), 60, 99
Sarah (Stapleton), 63, 103.
Seth, 46, 48, 60. 99
Seth, Jr, 41, 46, 47, 59.
Seth Austin 61. 100.
Seth Packard, 62.
Susan Uhl, 48, 61.
Thomas James, 48.
Walter, 105
Warren C, 65
William B, 65
William Denison, 48, 62, 102
William Emerson, 62.

Baker,
Birdie Burroughs, 129.

Baldwin,
John Denison, 160.
Jonathan, 22

Bannon,
Edward J, 80. 118
Ida (James), 80, 118.
Sarah Marcella, 80, 118

Barber,
Col Levi, 26

Barker,
Anna, 24.

196

Captain, 39.
Isaac, 24, 33.
Joseph, 24, 25
Judge, 28.
Michael, 24
Nancy, 24.
Rhoda, 24
Timothy, 24
William, 24

Barnes,
Mary, 109.

Battelle,
Colonel, 17, 22, 23.
Cornelius, 23
Ebenezer, 22, 23
Louise, 23
Thomas, 23.

Baxter,
Bessie Inez, 139
Sarah (Boardman), 139.
Wilson, 139

Bazler,
Charles, 115.
Ida (Johnson), 115
Oakland F., 115.
Seward All, 115.

Beard,
Rebecca Emma, 90.

Bennett,
Sarah A., 78.

Bent,
Daniel, 29.
Dorcas, 29.
Nahum, 29
Silas, 29.

Betts,
Albert, 69
Julia, 69
Laura, 69.
Nancy (Hurst), 69.
Thomas, 69
Uriah, 69.

Billings,
Ebenezer, 159.
Joseph, 160
Roger, 160

Blennerhasset,

Harman, 36

Boardman,
Bailey, 103.
Bessie, 103.
Burton, 103
Lewis, 103, 139
Sarah (Bailey). 103 139
Sarah Grace 103, 139

Bolton,
John, 188.

Books,
David, T, 81, 120
Frank E, 81. 120.
Harry S, 120.
Kate (Froblet), 120
Linnie May, 81, 120
Maria (Miller). 81, 120
Mary Flora, 81.
Oscar E., 81, 120
Samuel H., 81, 120.

Borodell,
Ann, 9, 154, 155, 170.
John, 155, 156.

Bradford,
Maj. Robert, 26

Breese,
A. M., 137.
Carl, 137.
Clara (Bailey), 104
Claude M, 137
Edwin Hatfield, 104
Hannah, 137.
Harriet (Talmadge), 104.
Julia M, 104
Julia (Shipman), 137
Lafe Budd, 104

Brigham,
W. I Tyler, 189.

Brisbin,
Helen Maud, 117
Norma, 117.
Stella Sampson, 117
William M., 116, 117.

Broadstreet,
Rev. Mr., 174

Brocamp,

197

Lissette, 74.

Brown,
 Arminta, 116
 Eliza (Long), 124
 George, 124
 James, Jr , 158.'
 John, 124.
 Margaret, 76

Bryers,
 Walter, 114

Buchanan,
 Frederic, 138
 Helen Hunter, 138
 John, 138
 Leila Margaret. 138.
 Lucy (Hunter), 138
 Margaret, 138.
 Mary Lorena, 138

Bullard,
 Asa, 14
 Eleazer, 14.

Bundy,
 Caroline (Paine), 59, 96.
 David Denison, 59
 Eliza Melinda, 59, 97.
 Hezekiah Sanford, 59. 80, 96
 Julia Ann Paine, 59, 96.

Burr,
 Aaron, 36

Burrows,
 Hannah, 160

Burtenshaw,
 Emma, 118.

Buswell,
 Hannah, 190.

Butcher,
 Benjamin, 64
 Charles, 64
 Frank, 64.
 Henrietta, 64
 Henry, 64
 James, 64
 Josephine, 64
 Lucy, 64.
 Margaret, 64
 Mary, 64.

Mildred, 64.
Nancy (Bailey), 64

Butler,
 Eva Elvira, 142
 Lady Ann, 164

Camp,
 John, 16

Campbell,
 Herman B , 118.
 Lizzie, 105

Carpenter,
 Frederick, 98.
 Louise, 101
 Mary, 98.
 Sarah, 98.

Carrick,
 Emma, 83.

Caumm,
 Estella, 137.

Chalkley,
 Rebecca, 6.

Chapman,
 Harriett, 61
 Isaac, 61.
 Mary, 61.
 Sarah (Perkins), 61.

Chenoweth,
 Mary, 65

Cherrington,
 Rev. Arthur Paine, 96, 109,
  134, 140.
 Betty (Denny), 134, 141.
 Charles Simpson, 69, 110
 Rev. Edgar Hurst, 69, 110
 Edith Clione, 96, 109, 134,
  141.
 Elizabeth (Paine), 96, 109,
  134, 140
 Ernest Hurst, 96, 109, 134,
  141.
 Ernest Hurst, Jr., 134, 141.
 Ethel, 110
 Frank, 110.
 Frederic, 110
 Rev. George W , 96, 108,
  109, 134, 140.

Harold, 110
Helen, 110.
Julia (Paine), 69, 109.
Laura, 96, 109.
Lemuel Bundy, 69, 110
Lora Eleanor, 69, 110
Mae (Elliott), 110.
Mary (Barnes), 110.
Maynard, 110.
Stella Janet. 96, 109.
Stella (Steele), 110
Wanita Grace, 96, 109, 134, 140.
William Douglas, 96, 109.
Rev William Douglas, 69, 109, 110
Rev. William W, 68, 69, 109

Chesebrough,
Abigail, 181, 187, 188.
Abigail (Ingraham), 171, 187, 188.
Anna (Stevenson), 183, 187.
Elisha, 188
Elizabeth, 188.
Maria, 187.
Nathaniel, 154.
Samuel, 183, 187, 188.
Sarah, 188.
William. 183, 184, 185, 186, 187, 188.

Chestnut,
Charles Sumner, 75, 116
Earl Acton, 75, 116.
James, 75, 115.
Jeanette Luella, 75, 115.
Katherine Estella, 75, 116.
Pauline (Johnson), 75, 115.

Choate,
Francis, 14.
Isaac, 14.

Claar,
Ripley C., 115.

Claggett,
Elizabeth, 100.

Clark,
John, 16

Coffman,

Caroline (Hawk), 91.
Claude, 91.
J. C, 91.

Cogswell,
Abigail, 24.
Daniel, 24
Job, 24.
John, 24.
Peleg, 24.

Cole,
Bertina Grace, 144
Bert Meno, 143
Cecil Gerald, 144
Chester Ray. 143
Clifford Bert, 143.
Earl Meno, 143
Grace (Kendall), 143
Harvey Leland, 144.
Walter Robert, 143.

Cook,
Andrew Clark, 44.
Bennett, 44, 45, 55, 56, 86.
Hannah (James), 41.
Hannah (Johnson), 45, 55.
Harriet, 45.
James, 45.
John James 45.
Capt Joseph, Jr, 42, 43, 45
Nancy, 42, 43
Pardon, 45.

Cooke,
Bennett, 56, 57.
Charles Hildreth, 56.
Clara Betty, 57, 87
Fanny M, 57, 87.
Frances V., 56, 86
Hannah, 56 86.
Harriet, 55, 85.
Henry C., 56, 86
Jeptha Kincheloe, 57.
Hon. John James, 56, 57, 87.
Julia, 57, 89.
Julia (Devol), 56, 86.
Julia (Kincheloe), 55, 85.
Laura, 56, 57.
Letha (Devol), 57, 87.
Maria, 56, 85
Mary F., 56, 86.
Mary James, 57.
Paul, 45, 55, 85.

Sarah, 55, 85.
Sophia, 57.
Sophia (Kincheloe), 57, 87

Cornell,
Murray, 145

Colton,
John, 183.

Couch,
James, 16.

Cowden,
Anna Hayes, 74.
Clifford Keely 74
Edgar H , 73.
Emma, 73.
Jennie, 73.
Mary Bennett. 73
Romaine (Rathburn), 73
Rev. Truman S., 73.

Crawford,
Clara (Welles), 127.
Cornelia Chapin, 127.
Harry, 127.
Welles, 127.

Crouch,
Elizabeth, 102.

Currie,
Hannah E., 77.

Cushing,
Elizabeth, 24.
Henry, 24.
Nathaniel, 24
Col. Nathaniel 17, 20, 24.
Sally, 24
Thomas, 24.
Varnum, 24.

Cushman,
Victor Nilssen, 136.

Cutler,
Manasseh, 11

Dalby,
Emeline, 94.

Dana,
Augustus, 27.
Betsy, 27.

Charles, 27
Edmund, 27
Fanny, 27
John, 27.
Luther, 27
Mary, 27
Stephen, 27
William. 27 28
Capt. William, 27.

Danielson,
Col. Timothy. 39

Dascomb,
Ella, 84

Davidson,
Elizabeth, 102
Helen Dudley, 102.
Joshua, 102

Davis,
Jonas, 32, 33
Sarepta, 81.

Deems,
Jane, 64

Denison,
Abigail, 160.
Agnes (——), 152
Amy, 160.
Ann, 158, 159, 160
Ann (Borodell), 147, 155, 156, 158
Avery, 160.
Borodell, 158
Christopher, 160
Daniel, 149, 159, 160
Maj. Gen. Daniel, 148, 149, 150, 151, 152, 153, 154
Desire, 160
Edward, 148, 149, 150, 152, 153, 159.
Elizabeth, 149, 152.
Esther, 7, 8 10, 37, 39, 146, 160, 161.
George, 149 151, 152, 153, 157, 158, 159
Capt. George. 9, 10. 39, 147, 148, 149, 150, 151, 153, 154, 155, 156, 157, 158, 160, 169. 172, 173 174
Hannah, 154, 160.

Hannah (Burrows), 160
Hannah (Tyler), 160
John, 149, 150, 151, 152, 153, 159, 160
Capt. John B., 158, 159, 163.
Joseph, 160
Luce, 152.
Lucy, 160.
Margaret, 158
Margaret (Monck), 148, 151, 152, 153.
Martha, 149.
Mary, 152, 158, 160
Nathan, 160
Phebe, 159
Phebe (Lay) 159, 160.
Robert, 159
Samuel, 159
Sarah, 153, 154, 159, 182.
Thankful, 160.
William, 9, 10, 148, 149, 150, 151, 152, 153, 157, 158, 159, 160, 182, 190.

Denning,
Dorothy, 120
Georgia (Miller), 119, 120
Leslie B., 120.
Leslie Burk, Jr., 120.

Denny,
Betty Clifford, 134, 141.

De Vaughan,
Laura, 64.

Devol,
Frances, 56.
Julia Maria, 56.

Devoll,
Barker, 24.
Charles, 24
Christopher. 24, 25.
Frances, 24.
Henry, 24.
Cap. Jonathan, 24.
Nancy, 24.
Sallie, 24.
Silas, 24.

Dewey,
Admiral George, 154

Dickason,

Cornelia, 92.

Dickey,
Fanny Mary, 62.

Dixon,
Alfred, 122, 123
George Alfred, 123.
Leonard Gold, 123.
May (Gold), 123.

Dodge,
Clara, 69.
John, 27.

Dole,
Whitten, 49.

Daugherty,
Draper Mallie, 119
Emily Belle, 119
Harry M., 119.
Lucy (Walker), 119

Douglas,
John Beverly, 100.
John Beverly, Jr., 100.
Julia (Bailey), 100.

Doyle,
Emilly (Hurst), 71, 111.
John H., 71, 111.
Lucile, 71, 111.
Petra, 71, 111.
Robert, 71, 111.

Dudley,
Patience, 149.
Gov. Thomas, 149.

Duling,
Elizabeth, 6

Dunham,
Daniel, 27.
Persis, 27.

Ebert,
Charles, 86.
Frances (Cooke), 86.
John R., 66.

Edmund,
Miss, 182.

Edwards,
Cornelia (Rathburn), 113,

145.
David F., 113, 145
David Frank, 113, 145.
Florence (Aughey), 143.
Herman C., 142, 143.
Jefferson R, 114
Lottie Cecilia, 143
Marie, 114, 145.

Eliot,
Rev. John, 148.

Elliott,
Esther, 136.
Mae, 110.

Ely,
Mary, 105
Victoria, 105
Wilson, 105

Emerson,
Caleb, 62.
Elizabeth Smith, 62.
Mary (Dana), 62.

Ervin,
Edgar Wells, 121
Ethel Fay, 121
Mary Adaline (Miller), 121.

Everett,
Harriet Anna Maria, 98,
136
John Ross, 98, 136.
Mary Shipman, 98, 136.

Farewell,
Jonathan, 16.

Fay,
Edna G., 145.

Fearing,
Hon. Paul, 20.

Fenner,
Arthur, 162.
Sarah, 162.
William, 162.

Fenwick,
Col. George, 164.

Ferris,
Doritha Lois 139.

Esther Annette, 139
Frank W, 139.
Mary (Walton), 139
Muriel Elizabeth, 139
Peter Francis, 139.
Virginia, 139
Walton Cutler, 139.

Finnell,
Ralph E., 128.

Fleehart,
Joshua, 30.

Foraker,
Arthur St. Clair, 97.
Clara Louise, 97, 136.
Florence M., 97, 135
Joseph B (Capt) (Sena-
tor), 96, 97. 135.
Joseph Benson, Jr, 97, 135.
Julia (Bundy), 96, 97, 135.
Julia Bundy, 97, 136.

Ford,
Reuben, 157.

Fowler,
C. E., 111.
Harold Doyle, 111.
Louise Hobson, 111
Lucile (Doyle), 111.
Margaret Ella, 111.
Robert Charles, 111.

Franklin,
Benjamin, 168.

Froblet,
Kate, 120.

Frye,
Louis, 138

Fuchoberger,
Minnie F, 143.

Fuller,
James, 66.
Lucy Matilda, 66.
Mary (Walker), 66.

Gace,
John, 151, 152.

Gibson,

Colonel, 82.
J. L , 65.

Gifford,
Jennie, 98.

Gilliland,
Edward, 126
Florence Bell, 123.
George Edward, 125, 126
Margaret Elizabeth, 126
Mary (Long), 126
Nellie, 126.
Pauline, 126

Gillespie,
———, 48.

Gillet,
Lucy C., 67

Gold,
Addie (Miller), 82, 122
Earl Samuel, 82
George Allen, 82, 122
George Leonard, 82.
Harriet Pearl, 82
Laura Jane, 82.
May Maria, 82, 122.
William Conrad, 82.

Goldsworthy,
Ethel Eliza, 144.

Goodale,
Betsy, 25
Cynthia, 25.
Henrietta, 25
Lincoln, 25
Maj Nathan, 20, 25
Sally, 25.
Susan, 25.
Timothy, 25

Gordon,
George H., 87.
Harry, 87.
Letha (Cooke), 87.

Graham,
Bessie M , 132.

Greene,
Griffin, 26.
James, 138.
Phebe, 26.
Philip, 26

Richard, 26.
Susan, 26.

Greenslade,
Joanna, 171, 173

Guthrie,
T., 27.

Hammond,
Eleanor, 87.
Fanny (Cooke), 87.
Frank L , 87
Frank Lloyd, 87.
James, 87.
Lillian, 87.
Mary Carr, 87
Sophia, 87
William, 87.

Hansen,
Charles David, 119.
Charles M , 119
Lucinda (Miller), 119
Norma Knight, 119

Hare,
Blanche, 71.
Claude, 71.
Dr. Daniel A., 71
Elizabeth (Hurst), 71.
Ernest, 71.

Harriman,
John C , 125
John Clifford, 125
Nellie (Long), 125.

Harrow,
Rev. John, 133.

Harwood,
Elizabeth, 49.

Haskell,
Capt. Jonathan, 26.

Hatcher,
Elmer L , 134, 141.
Paul Cherrington, 134, 141.
Robert James, 134, 141
Wanita (Cherrington), 134, 141.

Hawk,
Amanda Eleanor, 57, 90

Caroline (Paine), 57, 91.
David Wilmot, 57, 91.
Eliza Ophelia, 57, 91.
Emma (Beard), 90.
Eugene Owen, 90.
Francis Asberry, 57, 90.
Francis Wilmot, 90
George Clifford, 90
Jacob W., 57, 90.
James Monroe, 57, 90.
Lillie Melissa, 90.
Mary E. 57. 91
Mary (Marriett), 90.
Melissa Abigail. 57, 90.
Melissa (Paine), 57, 90.
Stella, 90.

Hawkins,
Elizabeth, 69

Hawley,
Frederika, 70

Hildreth,
Doctor, 11, 17.

Hitchcock,
Albert C., 108.

Hite,
M. P., 105.

Hoffman,
Arthur Sullivant, 67, 106.
Charles Bardwell, 51.
Cornelia Virginia, 51, 67.
Daniel, 42, 50, 66, 106
Maj. Daniel Webster, 51, 67,
68, 108.
David Allen, 51, 67, 106.
Douglas Ripley, 68.
Edgar Brown 67, 107
Edith Frances, 106.
Edith Francis, 140.
Effie Louise, 67, 107.
Emily (Smith), 67, 106.
Florence Delano, 68, 108.
Frank Ferno. 66
Frank (Watterhouse), 106,
140.
Harry Brown, 66.
Helen, 140.
James Fuller, 66, 105, 106,
140.
John Adams, 67, 107.

John James, 50
Josie (Miles), 140.
Julia (James), 50, 66
Lucy (Fuller), 66, 105
Lucy (Gillett), 68 108
Lyne Starling Sullivant, 106
Mary Ely, 106
Mary (James), 106.
Mary (Sullivant), 67, 106.
Ripley C, 106, 140.
Ripley Christian, 51, 66, 67,
105, 106, 107.
Victoria (Ely), 106
William Gillett, 68.

Holman,
Mabel Cassire, 8, 172.

Holmes,
Joshua, 171, 188.

Horne,
Mary Margaret, 102.

Hover,
Blanche C., 91.
Clarence A, 91
David F., 91.
Mary (Hawk), 91.

Hoyt,
Ezra, 27.

Humphrey,
Emma, 41.

Hunter,
Anna Harriet, 101.
Carrie, 100, 138.
Charles Robert, 100.
Howard Bailey, 101.
James, 61.
Lucy Lorena, 101, 138
Martha Aurelia, 100, 138.
Mary Annette, 100
Nellie, 101.
Robert M, 100, 138.
Sarah (Bailey), 100, 138.
Sarah Ethel. 101.

Hurlburt,
Benoni, 28.

Hurst,
Amanda, 59, 95.
Bessie (Graham), 132.

Carl, 71.
Carl L , 95, 132.
Caroline E., 94.
Caroline L , 58, 94.
Carrie Grace 94
Catherine (Little). 95, 132
Charles, 71.
Charles B , 59, 95, 133.
Charles S , 132
Clara (Dodge), 69.
Clinton, 70.
Clyde W , 94. 131.
C. Scott, 94. 131, 132.
David L , 58, 93, 94, 130.
Denison, 51, 70
Dewitt W , 132.
Douglas T , 59, 95, 133.
E. Corlene, 133.
Edith, 71.
Eliza, 58.
Elizabeth, 71
Elizabeth Cecilia, 51, 71
Elizabeth (Hawkins), 70.
Elizabeth (James), 51, 68
Ella (Patterson), 94, 131
Ella (Warner), 95, 133.
Elwin L., 95, 132.
Emeline (Dalby), 94, 130.
Emily Lucretia. 51, 71.
Ethel M., 95, 133.
Eugene, 70.
Flora, 69.
Florence (Morrison), 133.
Frances (Remington), 132.
Frederic A., 132.
Frederika (Hawley), 71.
George, N , 95.
Gilbert S., 95, 133.
Harry, 71.
Harry Alkire, 132
Helen J , 131
Hooper, 51, 68.
Hortense (Asbaugh), 131.
Jeanette M , 133
J. M., 132.
John, 70.
John A , 132
John Nelson, 58, 93
John Rathburn, 51, 69.
Joseph M , 58, 74, 95 132.
Joseph N , 94
Julia Ann, 51, 59, 69.
Laura (Morrow), 95, 133.

Lemuel J , 95 132.
Levi James. 51, 69.
Louisa Hermione, 51, 71.
Lulu Catherine, 94.
Luther, 70
Madge, 70
Marguerite W , 133
Mary, 69, 70
Mary Katheryn, 132.
Mary Louise, 131
Mary (Rockwell), 71.
Mary (Trimble), 70
Maud, 70
Maynard, 131.
Mellie, 94, 131.
Minnie, 69.
Myrtle, 95, 133.
Nancy, 51, 69.
Olive (Alkire), 132.
Pauline, 131.
R. Harold, 95
Robert. 132
Roy W , 95, 133.
Samuel H. (Gen). 51. 70,71
Sarah (Paine), 58, 93
S Louise, 94.
William, 71
William Fletcher, 51, 71
Wilson R , 58, 94, 131.

Hutchinson,
    Ann, 148

Ingraham,
    Abigail, 187
    Mary, 188
    William, 188.

Jackson
    Tho. as J., 88.

James,
    Abel, 5.
    Abigail, 24, 41, 45, 161.
    Anna, 23, 40, 41, 161.
    Chalkley, 6.
    Ripley Currie, 77, 117.
    Charles Curtland, 53, 77, 78,
        117.
    David M. 53, 76.
    Edmund J., 6.
    Edward Mitchell, 53, 79.
    Eliza, 44, 54
    Elizabeth, 44. 51.

Eliza Elizabeth, 53, 79
Elmer Clinton, 79
Esther, 23 40, 48, 161.
Esther (Denison), 13, 40, 41
Florence Edna, 79
Franklin, 53, 79.
Grace Ella, 79, 117
Hannah, 24, 40, 44, 161.
Hannah (Currie), 77, 117.
Harmeon, 44, 54
Ida May, 53, 80
Janet (Mitchell), 117
Capt John, 5, 6, 7 8, 10, 13,
   14, 23, 36, 37, 38, 39, 40,
   41, 46, 146 160, 161
John (Jr., Hon , Maj), 5, 6,
   7, 24, 33, 34, 35, 40 42, 44,
   49, 53, 72, 78, 161
John Denison 44, 52, 53, 76,
   78.
John Ripley, 53, 76
Julia, 44, 50
Lydia, 6.
Margaret, 6
Margaret Eveline, 117.
Mary Beatrice, 79.
Mary Denver, 106
Mary Eleanor 53, 79.
Matiller, 53
Nancy, 44, 50.
Nancy (Cook), 44, 49.
Nancy Cook, 53, 76.
Oota Bell, 79
Philip, 6.
Polly, 24, 40, 46, 161.
Ripley Currie, 77, 117.
Roanna, 44, 51
Samuel, 161.
Sarah, 79.
Sarah (Bennett), 79, 117.
Sarah (Mitchell), 53 76
Silas Edward, 79.
Simeon, 24, 40.
Susannah, 7, 23, 40 41, 161.
Thomas, 24, 40, 161
Thomas Denison, 53 76
Tryphena, 53, 80.
William, 6 14, 16, 24, 40,
   41, 44, 161
William B , 6.
Zachariah Ragon, 53, 78, 79,
   117.

Jeffrey,
   George, 137.
   Harriet (Everett), 137.
   Phineas Cicero, 136, 137.
   William Everett, 137.

Johnson,
   Adelia, 52
   Benjamin, 44.
   David Todd, 75, 115
   Dr Elihu, 51 52, 74
   George W , 52, 74, 75, 115.
   Hershal V. 75, 115
   Ida B , 75, 115.
   Joseph, 75.
   Julia Ann, 63
   Julia James, 52 76
   Leonidas, 52.
   Lucretia, 52, 75
   Mary (Ridgeway), 75, 115
   Pauline, 52, 75.
   Roanna (Rathburn), 52, 74.

Jones,
   Charles W., 124
   Miles, 79.

Kahley,
   Charles L., 126.
   Christopher F., 126.
   Dunham M., 126.
   Liuza (Long), 126.

Karshner,
   Donald B , 120.
   James, 120
   Linnie (Books), 120.

Kendall,
   Grace Ellen, 112, 143.
   Joseph Floyd, 143.
   Joseph Miller, 112, 143
   Minnie (Fuchoberger), 143
   Roanna (Throckmorton),
      112, 143.
   Rev. William, 112, 143.
   William J., 113.

Kerr,
   George, 28.
   Mathew, 28.

Kibbee,
   Elizabeth, 107.

Grace (Long), 107.
John L , 107.
John Long, 107.

Kincheloe,
Jeptha, 55, 56
Julia A , 55.
Sophia K , 56

Knowles,
James, 27.

Koon,
Minnie A , 111

Lafaber,
Donald J , 127
Eliza (Long), 127
Ella Grace, 127.
Harry, 127.
Harry Frank, 127
Margaret Catherine, 127

Lamb,
Robert, 101.
———, 101

Lay,
Phebe, 158, 162, 163.
Robert, 158, 162, 163.
Sarah (Tully), 162.

Levins,
Betsy, 27.
Esther, 27.
Fanny, 27.
John, 27.
Capt. John, 27.
Joseph, 27.
Matilda, 27.
Nancy, 27.

Lewis,
Cora, 64.
Perry, 64.

Lincoln,
Joseph, 27.

Little,
Catherine S., 94.
Nathaniel, 25.

Livingston,
Governor, 23.

Lloyd,
Bertha Doyle. 111
Marian Frazier, 111.
Petra (Doyle), 111
Petra Jane, 112
William F , 111.

Long,
Amanda, 55, 83.
Amanda L.. 83, 124.
Andrew, 54. 55, 83
Andrew A , 83, 125
Charles A., 84, 126
Charles C , 84.
Cornelia (Hoffman), 67, 107
Cornelia V., 84. 126.
Cornelia Virginia, 67, 108.
Daisy, 84.
Edna, 83
Effie Alice, 83, 124.
Elias, 55, 83, 124.
Elizabeth Lena, 83, 125
Eliza Flora. 84. 127
Eliza James, 83 124.
Eliza (James), 54 55. 83
Ella (Dascomb), 84, 126.
Emma (Carrick), 83, 124.
Fanny, 67.
Frank J , 84, 127
Grace Correll 67, 107.
Gwendolyn Frances, 127.
Harry Bertis, 107.
Harry Hoffman, 67, 107.
Helen Maxine, 127.
Herbert, 67
Howard J., 84.
Jacob A., 55, 84, 126
James Denison, 84.
John F., 84
John James, 55, 84, 126.
John L., 67, 107.
Lilly Dale, 83, 124.
Luiza E , 84, 126
Mary Frances, 83, 125
Nellie Boles, 83, 125.
Sarah (McNeil), 84, 126.
Stella Marie, 67, 107.
Stella (Shack), 127
Susan (McClure), 107
William, 84.
Mr., 26.

Lonta,
Delia, 74.

Loring,
Bathsheba, 25
Charlotte, 25
Daniel, 25.
Israel, 25
Jesse, 25, 26
Luba, 25
Polly, 25.
Rice, 25, 26.

Lovett,
Mary, 189.

Lucas,
Clifford, 114
Earl, 114.
Eliza (Rathburn), 74, 114
George, 74, 114
Gwendolyn (Simpson), 114.
Mary, 74.
Raymond, 114.

Lyons,
John, 99.

McCluer,
Anna Elizabeth, 129.
Annie (McKinney), 129.
Birdie (Baker), 129.
Charles Forrer Anderson, 89
Clara (Cook), 89, 129.
Daisy (Stork), 129.
Earl Hamilton, 89.
Henry Randolph, 89, 129.
James Steele 89, 129.
John Cameron, 89, 129.
John Grigsby, 89, 129.
Judge John Grigsby, 87, 89,
129.'
Julia Thompson, 129.
Lawrence Moss, 89.
Mary Cooke. 89
Mary (Thompson), 129.
Virginia Cook, 129.

McClure,
Andrew, 60.
Mary (Devol), 60
Sarah Devol, 60.
Susan, 107.

McCurdy,
John T., 116.

McDonough,
Joseph, 178.

McDowell,
Mary, 188

McElroy,
Rev. E. L , 110.
Enid Cherrington, 110
Jean, 110.
Lillian, 111.
Lora (Cherrington), 110.
Mildred, 110.

McGhee,
Susan, 119.

McKinney,
Annie Laurie, 129.

McNeil,
Sarah, 84.

Marriott,
Mary A , 90.

Martin,
Lena F., 79, 118
Mary (James), 79, 118.
Samuel G , 79, 118.
Susanna, 6.

Mason,
Amy Blanch, 122.
Capt John, 9, 155, 157, 164,
174.
Rebecca, 188

Mathews,
Doctor, 27.

Mathias,
Henry, 99.

Matthews,
Caroline Paine, 135.
Florence, 135
Florence (Foraker), 135.
Foraker, 135
Mary Ann Randolph, 135
Randolph, 135

Mattoon,
Arthur Maxwell, 103.
Arthur Maxwell, Jr., 103.
Edith, 103.
Eliza (Bailey), 103.

Winifred, 103

Mayo,
    Daniel, 22

Medert,
    Elizabeth, 120

Meeks,
    Isaac, 16.

Merritt,
    Capt. A J, 99.

Messenger,
    Amanda (Long), 125
    Dr Asa C, 124, 125
    Emily, 125
    Harold, 125.
    Lois, 125

Miles,
    Benjamin Buckminster, 26
    Capt. Benjamin, 26.
    David E, 140.
    Hubbard, 26.
    Josie, 140
    Polly, 26.
    Tappan, 26.
    William, 26.

Millar,
    Austin, 66.
    Cornelius, 50, 65
    Cornelius Elton, 50, 65, 66.
    Elton, Jr., 66
    Franklin, 66.
    Jane, 50, 65.
    Jessie, 66
    Julia Ann, 50, 65.
    Kate, 66.
    Mary (Chenoweth), 66.
    Nancy (James), 50, 65
    Rebecca, 50, 65
    William, 66

Miller,
    Addie, 54, 82
    Alexander, 54, 80.
    Alonzo, 54, 81, 82, 121.
    Amy (Mason), 122.
    Avery Floyd, 122.
    Barbara, 54
    Bertha May, 82, 121
    Besse Elizabeth, 81.

    Caroline Bundy, 82, 122.
    David Allen, 82, 119, 122.
    Capt. David Allen, 54, 80, 81, 119
    David Eben, 122.
    Edward, 54
    Elizabeth Cleo, 122
    Elizabeth (Rooke), 82, 121.
    Elizabeth Rooke, 82, 122
    Emily, 54, 80
    Emily Annette, 82, 121.
    Georgia, 81, 120.
    Harmeon (James), 54, 80.
    Jesse Jerome, 82.
    Joseph, 35.
    Lucinda Jane, 81, 119
    Lucinda (Rathburn), 81, 119
    Maria, 54, 81.
    Mary Adaline, 82, 121.
    Mary E, 54, 80.
    Mary May, 81, 119
    Mary Pauline, 122
    Ruth Caroline, 122
    Sarepta (Davis), 81.

Miner,
    Ephraim, 181.
    Hannab, 181.
    Joseph, 181.

Minor,
    Lieutenant, 173.
    Mary, 188.
    Samuel, 159.
    Thomas, 174

Mitchell,
    Hon. David, 52, 53
    Janet Dodge, 117.
    Sarah, 52, 53.

Monck,
    Margaret, 151, 152.

Morgan,
    James, 174.

Morrison,
    Charles, 128.
    Rev. Charles, 133.
    Florence J., 133.
    Juliette Corinne, 128.
    Juliette (Van Winkle), 128
    Rozalie Zell, 128

Morrow,
  George, 94
  Laura, 95
Mott,
  Captain, 39
Munsell,
  Leander, 29.
  Levi, 29.
Newell,
  James Edward, 130.
Newport,
  Newton, 114.
Oaks,
  Joel, 29.
Ohler,
  Clara (Paine), 58, 93.
  Elizabeth Roby, 93.
  James Oswell 93.
  Katharine, 93
  Willard Paine, 93.
Oliver,
  Alexander, 28
  Col. Alexander, 28.
  Betsy, 29.
  David, 28.
  John, 28.
  Launcelelot, 28.
  Lucretia, 29
  Mary, 29.
  Mehala, 29.
  Sally, 29.
Packer,
  James, 182
Paine,
  Abigail (James), 45, 57.
  Alice (Wilcox), 92, 130.
  Bennett Roby 58, 92, 130.
  Caroline, 46, 59
  Clara May, 58, 93
  Cornelia (Dickason), 92, 130
  David, 46.
  Judge David, 45, 46, 57.
  David Sanford, 53, 92.
  Delia Elizabeth, 58, 93.
  Eliza, 46.

Elizabeth Ophelia, 59, 69,
  96, 108.
Elizabeth (Roby), 58, 91.
Fannie (Allen), 92
Fannie Elizabeth, 92, 130
Howard Shepard, 92, 130
James Basil 58, 91, 92, 130.
Jonathan Douglas, 46, 59,
  68, 69, 95. 108
Joseph Arthur, 92.
Julia (Hurst), 59, 69, 95,
  108.
Kate (Richmond), 130.
Laurence Wilcox, 93
Lemuel Shepherd, 46, 58, 91
Mary Caroline 58
Melissa, 46, 57.
Sarah, 46, 58
Thomas Denison, 46.
William, 92.
William Denison, 58, 93.
Palmer,
  Daniel, 159, 182.
  George, 160
  Gersham, 158.
Palmes,
  Ann (Humphrey), 181.
  Samuel, 181.
  Susannah, 181.
  William, 181.
Parker,
  Cecil, 133.
Patterson,
  Benjamin, 27, 28.
  Ella, 94.
Peckham,
  Lydia, 6.
Perrine,
  America Virginia, 113.
Perry,
  Newton, 100.
Peter,
  Captain, 39.
Pfister,
  Adalyn Louise, 122.
  Elizabeth (Miller), 122.
  Harry R., 122.

Phelps,
  Dr. Charles, 160
Phillips,
  Elizabeth, 64
Pickering,
  Timothy, 28.
Pierce,
  Isaac, 25.
  Joseph, 25.
  Phebe, 25
  Samuel, 25.
Pixley,
  Elijah, 29.
Plumer,
  Jonathan, 27
Potts,
  Carrie (Hunter), 138.
  George W, 138.
  Joseph, 138
  Lennard Hunter, 138.
  Nancy, 138.
  Neva Lucretia, 138.
  William, 181.
Prentice,
  Sarah, 158
Putnam,
  A. W., 25.
  Ezra, 16.
  George, 29.
  Col. Israel, 22, 29.
  Gen. Rufus, 11.
  William Pitt, 25.
Quaintance,
  C. L., 116.
  Dale B, 116
  Gladys, 116.
  Hazel M., 116.
  Ida (Sampson), 116.
  Russel Sampson, 116.
Rathburn,
  Charles, 52.
  Charles B, 74, 114.
  Cornelia Virginia, 73, 113
  Delia (Lonta), 74, 114.
  Eliza, 52, 74.

Harriet, 52.
Harriet Cooke, 72
Ida, 74, 114
John, 52, 72, 73, 113.
Dr John W, 51, 52, 72
Joseph, 52, 73, 74
Lucinda, 80.
Minerva (Tomlinson), 73,
  113.
Ripley, 73.
Roanna (James) 52, 72.
Romaine, 52, 73.
Remington,
  Frances T., 131.
Rice,
  Maj. Oliver, 26
Richardson,
  Annie, 182.
Ridgeway,
  Mary Ann, 75.
Robbins,
  Charles, 64.
Roby,
  Elizabeth, 58.
Rockefeller,
  John D, 172.
Rockwell,
  Mary, 71
Rogers,
  Captain, 16.
  ————, 107.
  John, 149.
Rooke,
  Elizabeth, 82.
Roop,
  General, 42
Rouse,
  Barker, 26.
  Bathsheba, 21, 26.
  Betsy, 26.
  Cynthia, 26.
  John 21, 26.
  Michael, 26.
  Robert, 26.
  Ruth, 26.
  Stephen, 26.

St. Clair,
  General, 11.
  Governor, 29.

Safford,
  Hannah, 189.
  Col Robert, 36.

Sampson,
  Ida Bell, 76, 116
  Maud, 77, 117
  Nancy (James) 76, 116
  Stella Myrtle, 76, 116
  Rev. William A, 76, 116

Sanford,
  Mr, 27.

Sargent,
  Algernon, 65
  Julia, 65.
  Minnie, 65.
  Rebecca (Millar), 65.
  Samuel, 65.

Satterlee,
  William, 182

Saxton,
  Joseph, 154.

Schadle,
  John F., 122

Schell,
  Mary, 128.

Schellenger,
  Bertha (Miller), 121.
  Dorothy May, 122.
  Oscar P., 121.
  Vivian Gail, 121.

Scott,
  John, 60
  Mary Ann, 60.
  Nancy, 60.

Seamans,
  Addie, 98.
  Almira, 98.
  Alvin, 98.

Seiford,
  Doctor, 115.

Shack,
  Stella, 127.

Shepard,
  Calvin, 29.
  Colonel, 29.
  John, 28
  R. O, 29.

Sherer,
  Dwight E, 117
  Maud (Sampson), 117.
  Samuel, 117

Shipman,
  Addie (Seamans), 99
  Annie Maud, 99, 138
  Arthur Bartlett 99, 137.
  Budie Emma, 137.
  Charles F, 60
  Charles Frederick, 98, 137.
  Estella (Caumm), 138
  Frederick, 60, 98.
  Harly Leroy, 99.
  Jennie (Gifford), 99, 137.
  Jennie (Thomas), 137.
  Joshua, 60
  Joshua Seth, 60, 98, 99, 137.
  Julia Maria, 60, 99.
  Julia Sloper, 99, 137.
  Lyle, 137.
  Maria (Bailey), 60, 98.
  Mary Sibyl, 60, 98
  Minnie, 99.
  Myrtle, 138
  Sarah (Carpenter), 98, 137.
  Sibyl, 60.

Simpson,
  Bailess, 76.
  Charles, 76.
  Eliza (Lucas), 74, 114.
  Fanny, 74, 114.
  Gwendolyn, 114.
  Herschel, 74, 114.
  Lucretia (Johnson), 76.
  Lucy, 74, 115.
  Maud, 74.
  Michael, 74, 115.
  Robert, 74, 114.
  William, 75, 76.

Sinclair,
  David B, 99, 100.

Ella Richmond, 100.
Hunter B., 100
John North, 100.
Lydia (Bailey), 100
Mary Gertrude. 100.
Rodney Boise, 100

Sloper,
    Byron, 98.
    Carrie, 98
    Mary (Everett), 98.

Smith,
    Dudley Hoffman, 108.
    Emily. 67.
    Florence (Hoffman), 108.
    Frank Dudley, 108.
    Stephen, 27.

Spangler,
    Jeanette, 115

Speelman,
    Effie (Long), 124.
    Elias M., 124.
    Gladys Pearl, 124
    Sanford R, 124
    Vance, 124.

Stacey,
    John, 16.
    Philip, 15.
    Col. William. 15.

Stafford,
    Rev. Edward R, 131
    Mellie Hurst, 131.
    Miriam Kenyon, 131.
    Thomas H., 131.
    Willis Lincoln, 131

Stanton,
    C. H., 181.
    John, 160.
    Samuel, 158
    Thomas, 154..

Stapleton,
    Eliza, 63.
    Joshua, 63.
    Sarah Jane, 63.

Steele,
    Stella, 110.

Sterling,
    Deborah, 181

Stevens,
    Margery, 163, 180

Stevenson,
    Anna, 183, 184.
    Peter, 183.

Stone,
    Augustus, 27.
    Benjamin Franklin, 24, 27.
    Betsy, 27.
    Columbus. 27.
    Harriet, 27.
    Israel, 27.
    Capt Israel, 27.
    Jasper, 27.
    Capt. Jonathan, 17, 24.
    Lydia, 27.
    Matilda, 27.
    Polly, 27
    Rufus Putnam, 24.
    Samuel, 24.
    Sardine, 27.

Stork,
    Daisy, 129.

Story,
    Rev Daniel, 23.

Stout,
    William, 64.

Strider,
    Caroline Fischer, 123
    Edith Bell, 123
    Eliza (Atkinson), 123.
    Fred Coffman, 123.
    Milton F, 123.
    Pauline Atkinson, 123

Strong,
    R. W., 90.

Sullivant,
    Mary Elizza, 60.

Swan,
    John 2nd, 160.
    Thomas, 160.

Symmes,
    Hon. Daniel, 29.

Symonds,
Dep. Gov. John, 149.

Symounds,
Harlackenden, 149.

Taylor,
George Hubbard, 125.

Thayer,
Cornelia (Long), 108
Harry James, 108.
Jennie, 128.
Otis A . 108.
Otis Long, 108.
Virginia Annette, 108.

Thomas,
Jennie, 137.

Thompson,
Alice, 154.
Bridget. 154
John, 154.
Mary, 129

Thornhill,
Frank T., 119

Throckmorton,
Alonzo Joseph, 144.
Alonzo Wellington, 72, 113, 144.
America (Perrine), 113, 144
Arthur Laureston, 113, 144.
Aurilla Emmeline, 72.
Cecilia Desire, 72, 112.
Ethel (Goldsworthy), 144.
Harriet Cecilia, 113, 145.
Harriet (Rathburn), 72, 112
John Raymon, 144.
Joseph, 72, 112.
Mary Ellen, 72.
Ralph Harrison, 113.
Roanna Maria, 72, 112.
Sarah Josephine, 72
Susanna, 113, 144.

Throop,
Zebulon, 14, 16.

Tomlinson,
Minerva, 72.

Townsley,
Eben A , 121.
Edna, 121.
Emily (Miller), 121.

Treat,
Maj. Robert. 157.

Trimble,
Mary, 70

Tully,
John, 162.
Sarah (Fenner), 162.

Tupper,
Anselm, 16.

Turner,
Julia (Cooke), 89.
Smith D., 89.

Tyler,
Daniel, 190.
Hannah, 10, 160, 189.
Hannah (Safford), 190.
Hopestill, 189, 190.
James, 189, 190.
Job, 189, 190.
Capt. John, 189
Gen. John, 189, 190.
Joseph, 189.
Mary, 190.
Mary (Lovett), 189.
Moses, 189
Rev. Samuel, 189, 190.

Van Meter,
Clara, 120.

Van Ness,
Mr., 61.

Van San,
Mr., 30.

Van Winkle,
Donna Fayvette, 128.
Hannah (Cooke), 86.
Harriette, 85, 128.
Henry Cooke, 85, 128
Jennie (Thayer), 128.
Juliette, 85, 128.
Mary, 86
Munson Cooke, 85, 128.

214

Rathbone, 85, 128.
Sarah (Cooke). 85, 128.
W. W., 86.

Wainwright,

Francis King, 136
Joseph Benson Foraker, 136
Julia (Foraker), 136.

Walker,

Anthony Burress, 80, 118.
C. Jay, 118
David Anthony, 80, 119
Emily (Miller). 80, 118
Emma (Burtenshaw), 118
Frank Edwin, 80, 118.
Guy, 119
Katheryn Belle 118.
Lucy Matilda, 80 119.
Mary Belle, 80, 119.
Maurice Raymond, 118.
Myrna Lucy 118.
Russell Anthony, 118.
Sarah, 182.
Susan (McGhee), 119.
William Burtenshaw, 118.

Walton,

Clara (Carter), 102
James Rencock, 102, 139.
Rev. James, 102.
Mary (Bailey), 102, 139.
Mary Emerson, 102, 139.

Ward,

Frances Elizabeth, 61, 101.
Dr. G. A , 61, 101.
George Rollin, 61, 101.
Henry, 61, 101.
Mary Annette, 62.
Mary Celeste, 61, 101
Orlando, 61.
Susan (Bailey), 61, 101
Walter Payson, 61, 101.
Dr. Walter, 61, 62.

Warner,
Ella, 95.

Watterhouse,

Aaron, 105
Emily, 105.

Frank C., 105

Wayne,
General, 34.

Welde,
Elizabeth, 149.

Welles,

Clara, 85, 127.
Edward Lyman, 86.
George A , 85, 127.
Harriet Aurelia, 85
Harriet (Cooke), 85, 127.
Julia Mary, 85.

Wells,

Eliza (Bundy), 98, 136.
Harry, 98, 136.
Harvey, 97, 98, 136.

Wheeler,
Martha, 160.

Whipple,
Commander Abraham, 25.

White,
John, 27.

Wierman,

Clifton James, 118.
Danner Buehler, 117, 118.
Grace (James), 118.

Wilcox,
Alice L., 92.

Williams,

Hannah, 65.
Isaac, 159.
Jane (Millar), 65.
Rebecca, 65.
Roger, 166, 186
Sanford, 65.

Wilson,

Charles C., 126.
Rev John, 183.
Minerva, 70

Wing,
Oliver, 29.

Winthrop,
    Governor, 164, 173, 175.
    John, Esq., 164, 184.
    John, Jr., 185.

Witherell,
    Daniel, 174.

Wood,
    Caroline (Breese), 104.
    Carrie Bailey, 104

Clarence David, 104.
Emma Bailey, 104.
Howard Bailey, 104.
James, 37.
Paul Bailey, 104
Rachel Bailey, 104
Rhuy Bailey, 104
Stephen, 104.

Wright,
    Simeon, 27.

CPSIA information can be obtained
at www.ICGtesting.com
Printed in the USA
LVHW082359121119
637193LV00006B/116/P

9 780343 159849